"Jackson MacKenzie so lovingly and transparently delves deeply into the trauma and sorrow that can stand in between us and our real selves. This groundbreaking, must-read book brilliantly and compassionately illuminates the path to healing. It is soul work at its finest."

—Avery Neal, MA, LPC, author of
If He's So Great, Why Do I Feel So Bad?

"A powerful and moving force for good, *Whole Again* is grounded in the author's own research and deep, knowing wisdom. Everyone should have this book on their shelf."

—Erin Falconer, author of *How to Get Sh*t Done*
and co-owner of pickthebrain.com

"I've read many books over the years about recovery from abuse, both self-help and clinical, and *Whole Again* is definitely one of the best. Though not a therapist himself, Mr. MacKenzie has done his homework. His descriptions of personality styles and disorders are not only accurate but also understandable. The book is filled with practical, well-researched, and well-organized suggestions to aid the recovery process. It's clear that Jackson MacKenzie cares deeply about the unique sensitivities of each reader. I love this book."

—Catherine McCall, MS, (ret.) LMFT,
author of the international bestseller *Never Tell*

"This is a great book for recovering from any trauma or difficult relationship, including relationships with Cluster-B personalities. As Jackson MacKenzie says, it's not what you think—it's what you feel. To thoroughly understand what that means, read this book. With this powerful information, anyone can become whole again."

—Bill Eddy, LCSW, Esq., author of
5 Types of People Who Can Ruin Your Life

Whole Again

JACKSON MACKENZIE

Whole
Again

Healing Your Heart and
Rediscovering Your True Self
After Toxic Relationships
and Emotional Abuse

A TarcherPerigee Book

tarcherperigee

An imprint of Penguin Random House LLC
penguinrandomhouse.com

TarcherPerigee with tp colophon is a registered trademark of
Penguin Random House LLC.

Most TarcherPerigee books are available at special quantity discounts for
bulk purchase for sales promotions, premiums, fund-raising, and educational
needs. Special books or book excerpts also can be created to fit specific
needs. For details, write: SpecialMarkets@penguinrandomhouse.com.

Library of Congress Cataloging-in-Publication Data

Names: MacKenzie, Jackson, author.
Title: Whole again : healing your heart and rediscovering your true self
after toxic relationships and emotional abuse / Jackson MacKenzie ;
foreword by Shannon Thomas.
Description: New York : TarcherPerigee, 2019.
Identifiers: LCCN 2018053138| ISBN 9780143133315 (paperback) |
ISBN 9780525505082 (ebook)
Subjects: LCSH: Self-actualization (Psychology) | Self. | Interpersonal
relations. | BISAC: PSYCHOLOGY / Interpersonal Relations. |
SELF-HELP / Personal Growth / Self-Esteem.
Classification: LCC BF637.S4 M264 2019 | DDC 155.2--dc23
LC record available at https://lccn.loc.gov/2018053138

Printed in the United States of America
13th Printing

Book design by Ellen Cipriano

Dedicated to
Granddad and Uncle Win

CONTENTS

PART 3: DECONSTRUCTING THE PROTECTIVE SELF

PART 4: RESOLVING THE CORE WOUND

Whole
Again

FOREWORD

Beautiful.

Jackson MacKenzie has written a beautiful book full of love, support, and grace that lights a pathway to healing the emptiness that can haunt anyone.

Jackson highlights that out of the ashes of hurts and life wounds, it is human nature to develop what is called *the protective self.* We create this hard shell to keep ourselves "safe" from feeling empty. The sad double-edged sword of this outer armor is that our core wound stays intact within the center of our being, and is never adequately healed. We even attempt to ignore its existence. Despite these efforts, we know it's there because when we stop running from it, we feel the quiet whispers from the wound as it calls out to us. It can be frightening to stop running and stand still in our discomfort, fears, resentments, numbness, or unsteady emotions.

Jackson asks us to listen to what the wound is saying. This feels counterintuitive, but he shows us that until we stop to compassionately notice the whispers, we will forever carry our wounds with us. As a fellow survivor of trauma, I have no interest in burying the exact poison that has the power to steal aspects of my life. Wounds must be fully healed, or we fall into the mere management of our symptoms.

In Jackson's first best-selling book, *Psychopath Free*, he zeroed in on the world of emotional abuse while being the target of a narcissist, sociopath, or psychopath. As a survivor himself, Jackson experienced the challenges of finding restoration after intense abuse. *Whole Again* is the outcome of Jackson's personal journey. The beauty within *Whole Again* is that it's not only written to guide survivors of abuse to find healing, but also offers a new path for those looking for an inspired approach to trauma recovery, emotional centering, and stress tolerance; how to regulate a high degree of empathy for others; and navigating through the temptations of avoiding life in all of its richness.

According to Jackson, the process of reaching our core wound involves addressing the faulty mechanisms we've constructed to measure our worth in the world. We do this while staying safely wrapped in unconditional love for ourselves. The emptiness of finding our personal value in false pursuits can be soul crushing. However, offering the deep love we long to share with someone special in our lives, but instead to ourselves, is life changing.

At the heart of finding wholeness, we experience the process of waking up from the numbness that often engulfs our hearts and minds. Jackson wants each of us to lose our defense mechanisms that keep our spirits trapped in this chronic state of blandness. We deceptively believe that this flatness is a safe place because becoming fully whole feels like too much to ask of ourselves after what we've lived through.

Jackson compassionately guides us from focusing on the external world that leaves us always longing for more validation, to shifting our attention to our internal space, where peace is not subject to the whims of others. This peace is sustainable through being kind to ourselves and living in acceptance of who we are and, most important, how we feel. We no longer run away from our emotions in all of the forms that avoidance can manifest. Instead, we lovingly embrace our feelings without guilt or shame.

Jackson graciously shares numerous gems of wisdom within his new book. One of my favorite takeaways from *Whole Again* is, *"When you restore your own inner light, you no longer require the energy of others to feel alive."* By following Jackson on this groundbreaking path he illuminates for us, we're able to feel alive, whole, and restored again.

Shannon Thomas, LCSW
Author of *Healing from Hidden Abuse*

The Feeling in My Heart

At the end of my previous book, *Psychopath Free*, I described a "tight feeling in my heart." It wasn't painful or sharp, just a constant numb, squeezing sensation. It started immediately after my first relationship ended, and I felt it for five years straight. All day, every day, from the moment I woke up to the second I fell asleep.

Therapy and medications didn't touch it. I tried everything: talk therapy, cognitive behavioral therapy (CBT), hypnosis, EMDR (eye movement desensitization and reprocessing), antidepressants, benzodiazepines, exercise, cardiologists, deep breathing, acupuncture, thyroid tests, endocrinology, special diets, vitamins, herbs, genetic tests, quitting coffee and alcohol. I tried relating to it as a little boy and asked him to stop hugging me so hard. Sometimes I'd get short bursts of excitement or hope, but nothing lasted.

It really bothered me that I couldn't figure it out. I never thought about my first relationship anymore, so what was the problem? I hated the idea of being permanently damaged from my first encounter with romantic love. So I worked extra hard to seem non-damaged. I aced my college courses, found a great job, started a website, started a non-profit organization, and published my first book.

The feeling was still there.

I continued pouring myself into my work and the website. I wrote two more books. I woke up every morning at six a.m. to write, energized and excited to prove myself to the world. I went on dates and humbly described myself as a list of accomplishments. When people complimented my success, I would blush and feel a burst of approval. And so I accomplished more things. I redesigned our entire website, spending months obsessively customizing it to be perfect for our members and staff. We went live with the changes and everyone loved them. I felt a burst of approval, but it didn't last long.

The feeling was still there.

I started spending a lot of time on my own, intentionally isolating myself so I could be with my imagination. During the summers, I spent nearly every evening out by the water, drinking wine alone, watching the sunset and dreaming of new book ideas. I imagined characters and plot twists, which slowly shifted into more grandiose fantasies. I saw myself waging an important battle between bad people (psychopaths) and good people (people like me, of course). I imagined a perfect partner appearing someday, to rescue and love me.

The feeling was still there.

Don't worry, everyone said, time heals all wounds. But that clearly wasn't happening. In fact, by any sane person's standards, it was getting much worse. But I didn't notice. I was too busy trying to prove I was happy. My therapist diagnosed me with PTSD (post-traumatic stress disorder) and avoidant personality disorder (AVPD), but that didn't mean anything to me. I was totally fine, except for that feeling in my heart. I had already analyzed and understood everything about my first relationship. The problem was external, not internal.

Then the hypervigilance set in. On the streets, I started noticing when people were walking too close behind me. Even if they were far away, I'd stop and move aside so they could pass me. In the supermarket, it felt like the world was closing in on me. Why did everyone need to be in the way with their stupid carts? And how about police sirens, why did they need to be so loud? Why couldn't everyone just go away and leave me to my fantasies?

Anxiety and depression came next. Insomnia woke me up early in the morning to repeated nightmares of a masked man hunting me down. Before long, I couldn't even breathe correctly. My imagination started to flood with my worst fears, a relentless barrage of terrifying thoughts and images.

I remember at a particularly low moment, I said to my mom: "I don't feel like a person anymore." She gave me a book about mindfulness called *True Refuge* by Tara Brach. She had recommended books like this to me before, but I knew mindfulness and meditation wouldn't help me. Those things were for people with mental problems. My problem was a *physical* feeling in my body. Mindfulness couldn't fix a physical problem.

She had earmarked a page, so I decided to just read that *one* page. And there it was. A story about a woman who described a constant tight feeling in her heart. After all of the doctors and therapists who gave me bewildered looks and best-guess diagnoses, here was a book describing *exactly* what I felt. I devoured the whole thing in a few days, and ordered several other books on the same topic.

This was the beginning of a very rocky yearlong journey. A lot of people in these books said forgiveness is the key to the heart, so that's where I decided to start. I was in a frenzied excitement—finally, a new hope to get rid of my heart feeling. I began enthusiastically declaring everything wrong with myself and inventing soft qualities in my ex that didn't actually exist. I tried to welcome him into my heart and got very frustrated with myself for failing.

My forgiveness theme was: *"See, I'm bad too."* The more energy I devoted to loving and forgiving this way, the more I felt this horrible sensation tear through my heart. It was *intolerably* painful. It woke me up in the middle of the night. A relentless feeling that said: *"You are bad. You need to admit you are bad. Everything you do is bad."*

What in the world was happening? I thought forgiveness was supposed to get rid of the heart feeling, not make it worse. I assumed this scary *"You are bad"* feeling was the truth because it was *so* strong. It forcefully convinced me it was the ultimate truth, and that I needed to listen to it. It convinced me that anything else was just me fooling myself. By this point, I actually desperately longed for the old tight numb feeling in my heart. Numbness was better than this.

But it was too late. The feeling was uncontrollable and all consuming. Without my hatred of the person who hurt me, all my boundaries were destroyed. I was filled with self-doubt and fear. I had no idea who I was. All I knew was that I was wrong and bad and needed to admit it. I felt inadequate, shameful, and afraid.

It took me quite some time to realize that this horrible, unbearable sense of "bad self" wasn't my tightness getting worse. It was an old emotional wound un-numbing itself. This sensation wasn't new to me. I remembered it from five years ago, right after my relationship ended. And the more time I spent feeling it, the more I began to understand why it got numbed out in the first place. This feeling was completely self-destructive. Our bodies are built for survival—so it makes sense that my body shut this feeling down, since I didn't have any emotional tools to heal it.

Our bodies are built for survival.

This time, instead of running from it, or pretending it was good, or distracting myself, I decided to stay. I stayed for six months. I stopped writing, backed away from my website, and stopped taking on new projects. Instead, I dedicated every morning and night to meditation and prayer. My mind-set shifted from "how do I get rid of this feeling" to "what *is* this feeling?"

Instead of hating the heart feeling, I found myself holding my hand over my heart when I walked to work each morning. I was changing the relationship that I had with myself, my feelings, and my body. This nurturing process slowly taught me how to care and love again. Forgiveness was a natural by-product of this process.

There is a new feeling in my heart these days.

It's not numb, it's not tight, and it's not intolerable pain. It's a flood of light, tingly energy that runs through my body like a river and calms everything. My old truth of "bad self" has been replaced with a new truth: that we are *all* worthy and capable of love, even if we can't feel it yet. My inner source of joy and peace has been restored, and all of the other strange personality transformations have melted away. My sense of humor has returned, food tastes good again, I can cry freely, I'm smiling in pictures, and I love being around people. I'm not trying to be some perfect nice person, I'm just my regular old annoying self.

> We are *all* worthy and capable of love.

I can practically feel my heart calling out and dancing: *"At long last, we have found each other. Thank you, thank you, thank you, thank you."*

I wrote this book for anyone struggling with perfectionism, codependency, attachment disorders, personality disorders, trauma, or the aftermath of an abusive relationship. Over the past few years, over private message and video chat, I've conversed with people suffering from these conditions. I checked in every few months to ask some questions and follow their progress. With their permission, I have shared their stories here (names and specific details have been modified to protect privacy). I hope their experiences can offer you insight and hope.

You have been trying so hard for so long, I know. None of this is your fault, but you are the *only* one who can do the hard work to change it. There is a way back to yourself—to the freedom you seek—and we're going to find it.

Introduction

Fracture

Human wholeness is often defined as the unity of mind, body, and spirit. Emotional abuse, rejection, and trauma fracture this union, because a false shame message gets stored in our body that disconnects us from the sense of being unconditionally loved.

Here's how it happens:

Step 1: You start out joyful and whole, able to freely love (and receive love). This is how we all start out. Some people don't ever recall feeling like this, and that's okay.

Step 2: You experience betrayal, trauma, abandonment, judgment, or rejection from a trusted loved one. There is considerable emotional chaos, a loss of control.

Step 3: A false *internal* shame conclusion is formed from the *external* experience of Step 2. "I am defective and somehow *caused* this to occur, because I am _____ [inadequate, worthless, crazy, et cetera]." This belief of inner defectiveness blocks you from your true self—your inner source of life and joy, the sense of being unconditionally loved. This separation is extremely painful. (This is also called the *Core Wound*, the *False Core*, the *Narcissistic Wound*, or *Toxic Shame*.)

Step 4: In order to protect you from being consumed by this pain, your body numbs it away (in the heart, stomach, throat, pelvis, and the like). This can manifest as emptiness, boredom, numbness, tightness, voids, aching, and more.

Step 5: A protective self takes over to disprove and distract from the pain. Its primary purpose is control and avoidance: to keep you numb and prevent the same pain from occurring again. Unable to generate joy from the true self, the protective self relies heavily upon external measures of worth to keep itself alive. It is "who you are"—how you view the world, even the lens through which you approach healing. (This is also called the *False Self* or the *Ego*.)

The root of so much emotional trauma and resulting behavior is this unresolved message living in the body, numbed from consciousness, and subsequently blocking our ability to attach and to experience genuine love. Everything else described in this book (neurosis, personality transformations, black-and-white thinking, mood swings, anxiety, attachment issues, depression) stems from that core wound.

Most of my early work focused on the behaviors and symptoms of sociopathy and pathological narcissism, in order to help victims of toxic relationships identify and protect themselves from abuse. This helped people identify the *causes* of their suffering, but it didn't help them *resolve* their suffering.

Traumatized individuals complain about strange sensations in their body: numbness, tightness, emptiness, nothingness, hollowness. Unable to describe or understand these feelings, they go to therapy and tend to focus on the resulting behavioral and psychological issues: people pleasing, depression, perfectionism, mood swings, isolation, excessive daydreaming, need for control, resentment, rumination, caretaking, substance abuse—the list goes on, and it's unique to each individual.

Recovery becomes more about symptom management than root cause resolution. It's akin to putting out buckets of water every night to catch the leaking rain, rather than fixing the hole in the roof. Eventually the buckets become full, so you're running around finding new buckets and emptying old buckets, feeling more exhausted with every passing day.

This is the nature of trauma. It keeps you distracted with bucket management so you never have a chance to look up at the hole in the roof.

This is not your fault by any means. At some point, the body locked your feelings away because they were too painful and intolerable to experience at the time. Your true self is still there, it's just cloaked by obscure, frustrating sensations like "numbness" or "emptiness" or "boredom." Those things may feel impossible to work with, but this book suggests that those sensations are actually the key to becoming whole again.

As I shared my writing in various communities devoted to abuse recovery, codependency, C-PTSD (complex post-traumatic stress disorder), and even cluster-B disorders (borderline personality disorder, narcissistic personality disorder, antisocial personality disorder, and histrionic personality disorder)—hundreds of individuals reached out to share their stories and experiences with me. I began to realize that despite our unique stories, there were some unmistakable patterns to our suffering. If we shared suffering, perhaps we also shared a path to freedom?

Everyone's path will be different. Mine involved a combination of mindfulness, therapy, and spirituality. I studied mindfulness from psychologists and authors like Tara Brach. I also explored the concept of core wounding from philosophers around the world, like Stephen Wolinsky, PhD, and Leslie Temple-Thurston.

When I began to share what worked for me, I found that it resonated with nearly every person who reached out to me—even people with afflictions completely different from mine. I also found that these same techniques worked for them, which is why I decided to write this book.

In *Psychopath Free*, I wrote about how I felt like I had been "disconnected from my true self." I had no idea what that meant at the time, or how to go about "reconnecting." And I wasn't alone. One of the most common phrases I hear from trauma survivors is: "I miss my old self"—the person who felt cheerful, loving, and fun.

But what if the old self hasn't actually gone anywhere? What if we just have some very stubborn messages living inside of us that block us from experiencing it?

When we're hungry, we eat food. When we're out of shape, we go to the gym. When we're tired, we go to sleep. But for some reason, when we're feeling unlovable, we analyze ourselves to death until we feel worse.

The more logical solution, of course, would be to offer ourselves love. But what if we don't know how? What if trauma and shame are blocking us from letting love inside? What if our emotions have been numbed out to protect us? What if a traumatic experience fractured our connection with our true selves?

Without love's soothing comfort and kindness, we're bound to stumble over and over again. We experience the world differently. Love becomes conditional, waiting for others to show their cards before we show our own. We think if someone loves us completely (or whatever other external fixation we have), we'll finally feel content. But even when we get what we want, it's never enough. Love is replaced by attention, vulnerability by validation, and affection by approval.

When love flows freely from within, our infinite source is restored and all other behavioral anomalies melt away. We can do this by working backward from the steps I listed at the beginning of the introduction, which is exactly what we'll do in this book. You may fear that you are too far gone or too broken to recover, but the truth is, *anyone can become whole again*. This book is asking you to take a leap of faith, to trust in something you can't feel yet.

PART 1

Tools

Daily Practice

There is no quick fix for this work. It requires dedication and commitment to daily practice, even when it feels like you're getting nowhere. These wounds are not resolved by recalling a onetime "ah-hah" buried memory like we see in the movies. It's not about searching your memories, but instead feeling your feelings. But your true feelings have been dormant for so long that you need to actually change the way your brain is wired in order to experience them. You cannot think or analyze your way into emotions. To make this shift, you have to start changing old patterns and habits. This does not simply happen overnight. It takes months or years of changing the channel. With time, this practice becomes more and more automatic until it is your new default.

Think about it like learning a new language. Can you learn a foreign language in a month? I can't. I took Latin for six years, and I can barely remember two words.

Fortunately, this experience is much more rewarding than learning Latin. But it does take a while, and it involves activating parts of your brain and body that have not been used in a long time (if ever). So please be patient with yourself. You wouldn't be expected to pass the final exam of advanced Latin on your first day of class. A bad day doesn't mean you're a hopeless failure, just like an F on a quiz doesn't mean you won't pass the class. If you fail or stumble along the way, a good teacher would offer you special care to help you better understand the material. In this case, *you* need to become the good teacher.

I can't offer overnight solutions to complex emotional issues, and I'd be wary of anyone who claims they can. What I *can* offer are tools, perspectives, resources, and practices that slowly start to modify the mind's old habits. Eventually the discomfort in the body will follow, opening up and releasing so you can find freedom.

Even though this takes a considerable amount of time, the one thing I can promise is a light at the end of the tunnel. Not just a makeshift work-around for symptom management, but actually feeling *good* at your core. My goal here is to meet classic psychology with a few alternative concepts: core wounding, the protective or false self, love, and mindfulness. Complex emotional trauma and shame have strange—but predictable—methods of operation. With enough practice and dedication, we can crack these tricky defenses and get to the root of conditions that have previously been declared "incurable" or "hopeless."

During this work, if you experience any intolerable emotions, triggers, anxieties, or depression, please immediately seek professional help. We are going to be exploring uncomfortable sensations, and therapists can be invaluable resources in guiding you through that darkness.

Mindfulness

In order to get started, we need to learn how to get comfortable with discomfort.

Mindfulness is not about clearing your thoughts, but simply noticing what's going on in a non-judgmental way. Identifying our own behaviors and habits is one of the most difficult things to do, because our behaviors are so familiar to us that they seem normal. For example, perfectionists might notice: "Wow, I'm so judgmental and controlling all the time, what a nightmare! I really should stop doing that and start being nicer." But they haven't yet noticed how *harsh* they're being with themselves in this interaction. So instead, they judge themselves further for being too judgmental, which only lowers their self-worth and makes them *more* judgmental.

To offer another example, codependents might enthusiastically jump into forgiveness, only to become angry with *themselves* for failing to forgive someone who treated them like garbage. Put another way, they're willing to forgive others, but they're not able to forgive themselves for their own feelings.

Mindfulness helps us become aware of our default thinking patterns, so we can start to realize *how* we think. The goal is not to try to stop thoughts or feelings we don't like, but instead to *allow* them to be there—without judging, changing, or avoiding them. This lets you build a friendly, curious relationship with the stuff going on inside your body and mind, even the stuff that feels awful.

The challenge with fear-based thinking is that our minds go into this super-rigid, analytical thinking mode, which causes more of the same thinking. Sort of like an infinite loop. So we say, *"Stop it, nasty thoughts,"* and then get frustrated or afraid when they don't stop, which just leads to more nasty thoughts.

Being gentle, kind, patient, and compassionate with the weird thoughts—like you would with a friend—starts to relax everything. It breaks the feedback loop. And if you try being nice to yourself and you're met with a voice that says, *"This is stupid, it's fake, you're just doing this to try to avoid the actual truth that you're bad,"* then you can welcome that voice too. The more comfortable you become with discomfort, the more the discomfort will reveal itself to you.

A lot of times, there is some part of us that feels defective or crazy or evil, so we hide this from friends, family, and even therapists. Because if other people think we're good, then we believe we're good. It's like going to the gym and pretending to work out so that people will think we're physically healthy. It's really that pointless. With mindfulness, it's important that we're 100 percent honest with ourselves, and the strange behaviors or thoughts that we push away. Remember, *everything* is welcome. You do not have to pretend to feel good or normal when there is a voice nagging you that you're not. In fact, *that's* the voice you need to get in touch with.

Various people or experiences might trigger this feeling of inner defectiveness. So you try to seem normal and unaffected by it, because you want to be normal. But that is *exactly* the feeling we want to explore. This work is not about keeping up appearances or securing external validation. It's not about stifling or distracting from the scary inner voice, but rather welcoming it so that we can finally explore and disarm it.

As we start to understand our own behaviors, there are going to be really difficult, painful feelings that surface. These feelings will take over and convince you that they are the truth. Mindfulness will allow you to acknowledge that they are real, but not necessarily true, so that you can continue walking through this pain without being consumed by it or distracting yourself from it. You are essentially developing a friendly, curious relationship with your own feelings (especially the "bad" ones).

I often see mindfulness and meditation approached in this way: "I'm thinking of kittens and rainbows, healing and processing my past, loving my inner child, it's all so beautiful, I'm crying." But then this horrible feeling starts creeping in and the sufferer thinks: "What the heck? I was doing mindfulness, why am I feeling *worse*?" Because what's inside is *not* kittens and rainbows. It is an unbearable sensation that we have subconsciously been avoiding since the moment it entered our bodies.

Language helps us to identify the feelings that come up in mindfulness. If you're suffering from trauma or psychological disorders, there's a good chance you don't even feel your true emotions, because you're being blocked from experiencing them. You know how some people have repressed memories that come out in therapy? Think of these as repressed feelings. By learning about these emotions and preparing ourselves to feel them, they won't be nearly as scary. Slowly, we make the transformation from "my body feels numb or weird" toward using *language* to identify the actual feelings.

Feelings are a lot more complicated than happy or sad. When it comes to complex trauma and personality disorders (in oneself or a loved one), I can pretty much guarantee you'll be getting closely involved with the following feelings:

- Inadequacy: You are not enough. Others are better than you.
- Rejection: You and your feelings are unwanted.
- Unlovable: No one could love you as you are.
- Fear: Someone (or something) is dangerous or harmful.
- Resentment: Indignation at having been treated unfairly.

- Jealousy: Envy about someone else's success or happiness.
- Worthlessness: You have no real value and are deserving of contempt.
- Guilt: You've done something wrong or bad.
- Shame: You (or your feelings) are wrong or bad.
- Powerlessness: You have no ability, influence, or control over a situation.
- Emptiness: You are not real, something is missing, you do not exist.

There are many great resources on mindfulness, so I'm not going to reinvent the wheel here. I highly recommend reading the following books: *Radical Acceptance* and *True Refuge* by Tara Brach; and *The Untethered Soul* by Michael Singer.

Here is the most important mantra I need you to repeat throughout this entire book:

More body, less story.

The mind's default protective reaction is to focus on the story. Many people dealing with trauma can repeat their story a million times in crystal-clear detail. With mindfulness, we want to shift away from the story and start focusing on the sensations in our body. As we do this, we may try to create stories around the sensation ("I must feel this sensation because of *X* happening in my childhood or because of *Y* relationship"). Again, just use your mindfulness to become aware of that storytelling, and begin making the slow move toward body awareness.

In his book *The Way of the Human*, volume II, Stephen Wolinsky even goes so far as to write: "The story as to why you feel what you feel is not important. When you get into explanations, stories, reasons or justifications of 'why,' then you are *splitting** off* from the experience itself. The story comes after the experience and it is a justification and a distraction. You cannot think your way out of the False Core–False Self because *it* is doing the thinking. Your mind is driven by it."

I want to be clear that telling your story after trauma and abuse can be very important and therapeutic. In doing this work, we are not in any way pretending that the story wasn't real or that we are lessening its impact. We are simply trying to explore *why* the mind latched so hard on to this particular story, and what it is trying to protect us from.

Personal Responsibility

If you can't handle me at my worst . . . I really commend and respect you for setting healthy boundaries for yourself.

—STEPH STONE

We cannot control how others think, feel, or perceive us. We cannot spend our energy saving or fixing others. And likewise,

---

* *Splitting* refers to the unconscious failure to integrate aspects of self or others into a unified whole.

we cannot expect others to save or fix us. We are the only ones capable of doing that for ourselves. We can seek therapy and/or support, but no one else is responsible for our feelings except us. This perspective guides us toward wholeness as an independent, loving human being.

A guiding principle will help you through this work:

My feelings are my own responsibility. The feelings of others are their own responsibility.

Some mental illnesses are caused by chemical imbalances. They require medications to stabilize. This is not true for personality disorders or the people they hurt. These conditions are the result of our minds and bodies doing mental gymnastics to avoid intolerable pain.

The main issue is that we're expecting our external world to change, and *then* we'll be happy. The codependent just needs to rescue one more person, the perfectionist just needs to accomplish one more thing, the cluster-B relationship survivor just needs to see their ex's new relationship fail, the borderline just needs a knight in shining armor to offer infinite sympathy for their pain, and the avoidant just needs to invent some more imaginary characters.

Then we'll *all* be happy.

Try it from another angle: the heroin addict just needs a little bit more heroin, then they'll be happy. That's complete nonsense, so why aren't the above examples also nonsense? If we truly want love and connection, we need to go through the hard work and pain required to change *ourselves*.

We live in a world where people want others to validate and accept them for exactly who they are, but once again, *external validation will not make you any happier*. We can't just end our journey at: "I have this issue, accept me the way I am!" It's not the world's job to do that, and if you go down that route, you're likely to end up disappointed.

Along these lines, personal responsibility is asking that your personal happiness be based on *you*. Only you. It has nothing to do with how others have treated you, or how you have treated them. It is asking you to switch the focus from external measures of worth, to internal ones. It is asking you to believe that *the most important thing in the world*, right now, is recovering your own ability to love.

Unconditional Love

Before I lose all of my skeptical, atheist, or agnostic readers with God talk, I want to be clear that this does *not* need to be a spiritual endeavor. I grew up without any spiritual background and considered myself agnostic for most of my life. So let's start with a more logical and scientific approach to unconditional love.

The mind (especially the ego) has a negative bias. It is scientifically proven to be wired that way to protect us, often activated after traumatic situations. However, we're not running away from lions in jungles anymore, so that old wiring is really no longer as helpful to us. We have these wonderful brains that can learn from mistakes and make future adjustments, without activating the old run-away-from-lion mode.

When we sit there ruminating, having anxiety, obsessing, shaming, and blaming—we are spending our hours and days on negative thoughts (90 percent of which likely never come to fruition). Negativity has accidentally become *our religion*. We're so convinced it's truth because that's what the mind wants us to think. We are taking the mind's placebo. We're stuck in it, and not even aware of it.

We worry so much that believing in something positive is just tricking ourselves, when in fact our skepticism and fear are already playing right into the mind's tricks. The mind convinces us that the negative stuff is the ultimate reality, and anything else is just fluffy nonsense trying to distract us from reality. And we fall for it almost automatically. Mission accomplished.

Happiness and freedom come from learning how to nonjudgmentally notice these tricks of the mind. Noticing its negative bias. Noticing how it is scoffing at the idea of something positive. The more we "notice," the easier and easier it becomes to experiment with "un-identifying" with it.

Again, this doesn't have to be a spiritual thing. You could practice it purely as a scientific endeavor. Here is my hypothesis: If you try noticing and un-identifying with your mind's negative bias, you may eventually discover some wonderful and calm sensations replacing the tension and agitation in your body. As that happens, you may notice that your thoughts naturally become softer too. You may find it easier to bond with others, make friends, let go of resentments, and enjoy your life.

You're not pretending bad things don't happen, you're not living in fairyland pretending everything is wonderful, you're not loving nasty people and hugging strangers. You're simply un-identifying with the part of your mind that says: "Bad things are happening *to me*. My life is *unfair*. I am being *betrayed* and *let down*." You can still notice bad things happening and protect yourself, but these negative thoughts just don't have anything to "land on" anymore. The inner victim and ego begin to dissolve.

The stories we tell ourselves matter.

The stories we tell ourselves matter. Our bodies listen and react accordingly. And the cool thing is that awareness and consciousness allow us to *choose* which stories we tell ourselves. We are the masters of our own destiny. Our default programming is "negative stories," but as soon as we're aware of this, we have the power to start changing it.

Choosing to follow negative thoughts of shame, paranoia, and fear is just as "real" or "fake" as choosing to follow thoughts of love, forgiveness, and freedom. The difference is, one set feels like garbage, whereas the other set feels very nice. If we go with the former, we're deciding to let our mind trick us into misery—which, rationally and logically, is a goofy thing to do. We have a very limited time here on this Earth, especially if you don't believe in any sort of afterlife, so the most logical thing to do is enjoy that short time as much as possible.

Finding Unconditional Love

Okay, skeptics may now skip to the next chapter because the rest of this one is likely to produce some eye rolls and sighs.

In the late summer of 2016, the feeling in my heart was getting worse and worse, despite my putting more effort into it than ever before—all of my old hope and optimism had been replaced by fear. Every morning I woke up from the middle of a nightmare, covered in sweat, heart squeezing, and feeling like the world was closing in on me.

Desperate to find some peace, I took a long weekend to visit the White Mountains in New Hampshire. There is a beautiful trail that follows a waterfall to the top, and you can climb right in the water. I've always loved being in or around water. It has a calming effect on me, so this seemed like the perfect getaway.

But even in this most peaceful place, the feeling in my heart worsened. The nightmares continued. I left feeling more drained than when I arrived.

As I was driving home, I felt hopeless. If I couldn't feel peaceful there, how could I feel peaceful anywhere? There was something seriously wrong with me, and it was only getting worse. The heart feeling would never go away. I had a problem with no solution.

I was broken.

I was listening to some horrible rap song from my sister's playlist, when I suddenly felt a presence smiling kindly and reaching her hands out, beckoning for me. She was so loving and beautiful, nodding encouragingly as I doubted her. She didn't care that I doubted. To her, there was no such thing as "broken." She loved me completely as I was, heart feeling and all. And suddenly, the long-constricted feeling in my heart melted away into softness I hadn't known in years.

You have to understand, this was all very confusing to a lifelong agnostic. My logical analyzing brain quickly took over again and concluded that I had finally gone insane—it was only a matter of time. And as I regained mental control of the situation, the familiar tight feeling in my heart came back.

"Hmm," I thought to myself. "So my heart likes being loved. It doesn't like being analyzed and judged and treated like a lab rat."

Weird.

From that point forward, unconditional love became the foundation upon which I based my healing. It is what I meditated on, trusted fully, and turned to for guidance. It is what got me from "thinking" love to "feeling" love, which my body was very resistant to. It softened me so that I could experience the truth in my body, without fear or control.

So whether it's Jesus, God, Allah, the Universe, Essence, Love, Spirit, Mindfulness, or a guy named Tom . . . it doesn't matter what you call it. As you go through this work, you need to find a source of unconditional love, because the whole point is that you're not correctly experiencing love right now. So many of these conditions are about being locked inside a protective world, thinking you know how to love but failing over and over again. Building a relationship with unconditional love allows you to get out of this mind-set.

This is not the higher power we ask for help on our homework, or to win the football game, or to confirm our political beliefs. This is the source that we ask for love when we are unable to feel it ourselves. It is always willing to give love. It is always there for us, especially when we stumble.

A lot of times, people have become stuck on an idealized view of love that they have, which is more about romantic obsession, saving or rescuing, self-sacrifice, attention and sympathy. They repeatedly seek out this "love" from other people, thinking if someone else just reciprocates it, then they'll finally be happy. But of course it is never enough, because the issue is *internal*, not *external*. So this is instead about exploring a different type of love, one that has nothing to do with other people. It is more calming and lighthearted.

This might not come naturally to you, and that's fine. All I'm asking is that you be open to it, because you'll need it. If you think it's stupid or silly, ask yourself one simple question: *Is what you're doing working?*

If you want to try the spiritual approach, just imagine a white light always dancing above you, smiling as he/she/it watches over you on this journey. Maybe he/she/it is shedding some tears of joy, excited that you're starting this journey, nodding encouragingly for you to continue. Start there, and see what happens as we move forward.

The goal here is to move from thinking love, to *feeling* love. You do not need to *do* anything to receive it. If your higher power convinces you to change your job, or reconcile with an abusive ex, or find a new relationship, or accomplish a new project, or be used as a justification for discrimination or otherwise mistreating others—that isn't a higher power. That is your ego enabling itself in the name of "God."

You could try to sit right where you are, without moving a muscle, and feel it flood through your body. Knowing that you are loved and accepted for who you are, right now in this moment.

Unconditional love is not "I receive love if I do good things." That is *conditional* love. If we received *conditional* love from a parent or partner, then it is natural to also start by seeking this same *conditional* love from the higher power. We think if we do everything right, or sacrifice ourselves enough, or heal enough, or apologize enough, or [whatever] enough—then we will finally receive the love. We'll finally be let back in. We may view this higher power as a punitive figure, or something to be feared. Imagine if your partner said, "Bow down before me and admit all your wrongdoings." You wouldn't call that love, right? Hopefully not.

We need to shift away from this mentality and explore a new type of love—one that we may not have experienced before.

Unconditional love says, "I am loved even (especially) when I stumble." For someone recovering from a cluster-B relationship, this means offering yourself love when you obsess over your ex or check their Facebook page. For someone with borderline personality disorder, this means offering yourself love when you have an episode of rage. For someone with C-PTSD, this means offering yourself love when you get lost in fantasies of revenge or justice.

It does *not* mean those things are healthy. It does *not* mean you should encourage yourself to keep doing those things. It does *not* mean you are excused from harming others without consequences. It does *not* mean you should expect others to feel sorry for you as you work through this process. It's simply an *internal* recognition that these are behaviors of someone who is suffering, and punishing yourself for that will only drive you deeper into the very condition you are trying to escape.

We find wholeness by restoring balance—pouring less energy into the mind, and more into the body and spirit. The body is filled with extremely painful emotions: guilt, shame, rejection, and fear. Many of these were numbed to protect us before the fracturing. As we ask our bodies to begin experiencing these emotions (slowly), we realize that it is too much for any person to hold. This is where spirit, or unconditional love, comes back into play.

Your spirit wants only joy and love for you, removing any obstacles to that goal. It is merciful and forgiving, even if you can't feel it right now. Most people are *born* with this intact, and they do not need to be "spiritual" to experience it. It is just the innate sense of being good, having purpose and joy for no external reason. Children raised in a healthy, loving environment are likely to be connected to their spirit, regardless of whether or not they were brought up in a religious setting. Just like children raised in a shaming, judgmental religion are likely to be *disconnected* from their spirits.

A college student could go out drinking and partying every night, scoff at the notion of spirituality, never pray in their life, and be connected to their spirit. They feel no shame or inherent "badness" about themselves. They are whole, even if they're treating their body like crap. Meanwhile, a spiritual person could abstain from all of those things, dedicate their life to helping others, and still feel like they are "not enough." They are disconnected from their spirit.

This disconnect happens when a message gets planted inside us that makes us feel separate from unconditional love. Certainly the conditions discussed in this book often lead us to be "disconnected" from our spirit, and usually the problematic message has been numbed out. I put "disconnected" in quotes because we are not truly disconnected—just harboring a false belief that makes it seem that way.

And from there, everything else is really just an attempt to compensate for that original separation from unconditional love—from our true selves. We think if we can just do X, then we will reconnect. Of course, it never seems to work out that way.

Spirit, or unconditional love, is simply the part of ourselves that nurtures us for no logical reason. If you become disconnected from it, it will always try to find its way back to you (sometimes in very uncomfortable ways), because it is who you *truly* are.

As we start to see how hard this loving force is working for us, we begin to remember what heartfelt love feels like. The heart is the gateway between these fractured parts of ourselves, and it is our key home.

PART 2

Identifying the Protective Self

When our true selves are rejected, betrayed, or abused by a trusted loved one (usually parent or partner) and we don't yet have the emotional tools to heal, it's common for a protective self to form. The protective self sees itself as separate from others. It becomes more of an observer of the world, rather than an authentic participant. The protective self is usually seeking external validation for proof of its worthiness. To save or be saved. To fill a void it cannot express, to meet an old unmet need. It is largely based around control.

This is one of the most difficult things to understand, and it's where we really need mindfulness to see what's going on, to truly see our own behavior. The protective self has probably had the reins for a long time. It's your natural way of thinking at this point. It is "who you are." You can't work on something that you're not even aware of.

The protective self convinces us there is nothing wrong with us, that we've figured it all out. It says: "The problem was caused by external events, and the solution will be found in external things." It is often disguised in an innocent, childlike, confident, cheerful, victimized, or heroic way. This illusion keeps us stuck in the same patterns. While it's true that there's nothing inherently "wrong" with us (in fact, this is the entire point of the book), the protective self is blocking us from experiencing the wounded feelings that actually need to hear that message.

Here's how the protective self works:

The wound is unfelt, blocked by the protective self. It takes an incredible amount of energy to maintain this makeshift solution. Since the inner world is damaged, the protective self keeps itself alive through external measures of worth: accomplishments, relationships, money, status, appearance, attention, people pleasing, being overly "nice," sympathy, sex, perfectionism, obsessing about an ex, stalking, approval seeking, alcohol, caffeine, drugs, grandiose fantasies, revenge fantasies, social media, blame, saving others, being saved, and resentment. (Do any of these sound familiar?)

When we tell the protective self, over and over again, "I'm fine! I'm good!" the wounded inner core doesn't hear or feel that. It's just the protective self growing stronger and stronger, as the wound fades into a numb obscurity, an invisible status quo. Traditional self-help techniques don't really work because our bodies have blocked us from feeling the parts of ourselves that actually need help. Feeling "good" is more about maintaining a high, not deeply feeling authentic joy.

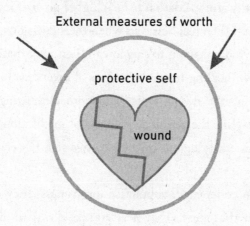

DISORDERED THINKING

External measures of worth

protective self

wound

This is why we feel unfulfilled by relationships, passions, and other important aspects of life. Sure there may be an initial excitement (or obsession) about a new endeavor, but it inevitably fizzles out. Because even when we get exactly what we want, it's all just hitting a protective shield. It is not reaching our true selves, so it never feels like "enough."

This is also why you can almost expect any spiritual or healing practices to fail, because it's not even contacting the part of you that needs help. It's just feeding your protective self. It is used as another external measure of worth. Perfectionists use it to become what they think an ideal spiritual person should look like, eternally seeking to be "good enough" for spiritual love. Codependents use it to dismiss their own needs and emotions, deciding they must rescue and help even *more* people in order to achieve selfless sainthood. Narcissists use it to start cults and show others how worldly and wise they are. Borderlines use it to seek sympathy and validation from a higher power for their poor decisions, and then feel betrayed when their decisions inevitably backfire. Avoidants use it to stay lost in their imagination, viewing their own healing through the lens of invented characters.

Observing the *way* in which we approach healing (or healing exercises, like therapy or forgiveness or meditation) is a great shortcut to identifying our own protective self. For example:

- When codependents practice forgiveness, they might decide that means they need to take down all of their boundaries, trust everyone, and have beautiful tear-filled reconciliations with the people who harmed them. They may even feel the need to apologize to people who mistreated them. Inevitably, they are betrayed or mistreated again and then wonder how the world could be so unfair.

- When borderlines seek out therapy, they might constantly revisit (or invent) sad sympathy stories. In conveying their lives as a tragic play, they are accidentally seeking the therapist's validation and comfort. They will have "breakthroughs" and "process" each trauma, but never actually seem to feel better.

- When those with C-PTSD meditate on the feelings in their body, they might try to "think" their way into these feelings. They use the protective tools they learned from their trauma (analysis, judgment, obsession) in order to label the sensations that they cannot feel: "I do *X* because of *Y*, so this feeling must be *Z*." By analyzing others and themselves, their protective self is still completely in control.

Stephen Wolinsky writes: "Any treatment to try to heal or transform a False Conclusion is a treatment, therapy or spiritual practice which is organized by the False Self based on believing the False Conclusion and, hence, can only yield a False Treatment, therapy or spiritual practice because the therapy or spiritual practice is being driven by believing in the earlier False Conclusions and premises."

So how can we become aware of this tricky protective self and break through it once and for all? The two clearest signs of the protective self are:

1. Focus on external things/people
2. A sense or compulsion that you need to "do" something

It convinces you that if you "do" this thing or if someone else "does" something, you will feel good. It could be accomplishing another project, doing drugs or alcohol, spending money, seeking a relationship, the list goes on. You can tell when someone is stuck in the trance of the protective self, because they say things like: "If I could just get that [raise/perfect relationship/deal/house/perfect body], then I'd finally be happy."

The protective self wants you to "do." In this book, I'm

encouraging you to stop "doing" and instead sit with the deeply uncomfortable, frustrating sensations that arise when you *don't* take action. To notice when that urge kicks in. And when we notice it, all we need to do is kindly decline what it wants us to do.

There is really only one way to diminish the protective self: *stop feeding it*. Instead we need to feel what's there when we *don't* indulge it.

But once again, the problem with protective selves is we usually don't even know we're stuck in one ("you don't know what you don't know"). Even as we're trying to analyze and heal, the protective self is still the thing *doing* the analyzing and healing. The faster we can gain this "meta-awareness," the faster we can get started.

Looking for Patterns

Patterns are a great way to start identifying the protective self. Imagine life is a movie that keeps repeating itself, over and over again. So the characters do the same thing, over and over again. It would be very boring to watch after a while. Now imagine the characters in the movie don't know they're in a movie. Instead, they are *you*, and they think the movie is reality. This is how protective selves work. They keep you stuck in a sort of infinite loop, constantly repeating and doing the same thing, unaware of what's really going on.

So what is your role in this movie? What storyline do you

keep repeating? Are you the damsel in distress, always looking to be saved and rescued? Do you keep ending up in abusive, unfulfilling relationships? Are you constantly dating narcissists, addicts, and other selfish people? Are your days filled with endless drama and crises? Do you always help people, only to end up feeling unappreciated and resentful?

Usually we play the part in this movie with other "actors" (protective selves). If our role is the victim, then we will need to find a perpetrator and a rescuer. If our role is the rescuer, then we will need to find ourselves a victim to take care of. If our role is an inability to take responsibility, then we will need to find someone who takes responsibility for everything. If our role is obsession with control or power, then we will need to find someone we can dominate. If our role is the polite selfless listening friend, then we will need to find someone who never stops talking.

To start moving forward, we need to shift our perspective from the eyes of the character to the eyes of someone watching this movie. The characters will happily repeat these stories and roles until the end of time. The person watching this movie might instead explore why and how the characters do what they do, and eventually change the channel, turning away from this boring movie.

Another important concept that Wolinsky describes is that "all False Cores reinforce themselves." They *intentionally* choose situations and people and thoughts that confirm the protective self's deepest fears, thereby justifying their own existence. For example, a codependent will continue to choose relationships and friendships with emotionally unavailable people, so the protective self can reinforce its belief that you are "never enough." People with borderline fear abandonment, and then go on to do things that *make people abandon them*. So the protective self is keeping you stuck in a trance, setting you up for failure so it can stay in control.

The following sections explore various ways to identify what's going on, to help you examine your own behavioral patterns so you can hit the "pause" button. Overlap is common—you might see yourself in more than one description.

Remember, this awareness must be kind. Please do not judge or hate yourself if you recognize yourself in any of the vignettes. Nobody chooses to develop a protective self. It stems from very confusing and complex wounding. It was an old protective mechanism, and you are on the path to heal it. This is not even who you are, so there is no sense in hating it. All that does is lock you in further. Becoming aware of the protective self is the first step toward healing.

> **Becoming aware of the protective self is the first step toward healing.**

People often don't want to see themselves in these categories, because they view these issues as an incurable life sentence or proof that they're defective or crazy. So they reject reality and learn to fake even more, driving them further away from their most authentic self (which paradoxically makes them behave *more* "defectively"). These conditions are all about avoiding a sense of inner defectiveness, so of course people are going to

Mindfulness/Unconditional Love

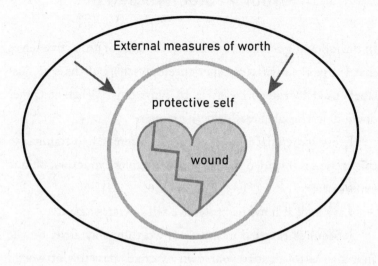

be hesitant to label themselves with something that seems defective. But rather than a label, I just think about it more as identifying with certain sets of behaviors and thinking, so that you can heal them. Pretending the problem isn't there will not solve the problem. I'm not asking you to take this on as your identity (quite the opposite, actually). I'm asking you to acknowledge there is a problem, so you can finally go about fixing it.

These things are not who you are. They are who the protective self is.

For now, all you need is to become aware of the protective self and have faith that there's something better on the other side. We're just adding one very simple addition to the drawing above.

Your Protective Self

In the following sections, I will describe a list of protective selves that I've worked with (or experienced myself), but these are just labels used to categorize a set of symptoms. When it comes down to it, the label really doesn't matter.

Every individual is going to react differently to trauma, so this section is intended to help you first explore your own unique experience.

Let's look at how the protective self operates again:

It requires external measures of worth to stay alive. So the first step is to identify your own external measures of worth. Below is a list of common ones. Circle any that resonate with you, and feel free to write your own.

Note: Any of these things in moderation may not be a bad thing. But the protective self doesn't do moderation. For example, there's nothing inherently wrong with "accomplishments." Someone could accomplish great things at work and be proud of them, then go home and live a happy life. But if "accomplishments" are an external measure of worth, the protective self will be constantly taking on new projects, obsessively laboring over them, fantasizing about them, imagining how others will react to them, ignoring life around them, and feeling discontent even when the accomplishment is a great success.

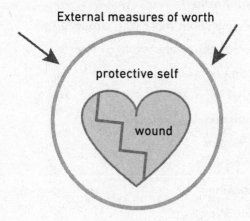

DISORDERED THINKING

External measures of worth

protective self

wound

EXTERNAL MEASURES OF WORTH:

- Accomplishing things (projects, work, and the like)
- Making money
- Social media validation
- Perfecting appearance
- Attention seeking
- Sympathy seeking
- Approval seeking
- Validation seeking
- Analyzing people (and the self)
- Diagnosing or labeling people (and the self)
- Being overly "nice"

- People pleasing
- Perfectionism
- Obsessing about those who wronged you
- Exposing those who wronged you
- Stalking or cyberstalking
- Alcohol
- Stimulants
- Depressants
- Sex
- Overeating
- Undereating
- Fantasies or daydreaming
- Revenge or justice fantasies
- Taking on battles of good versus evil
- Fantasies of unlimited love and adoration
- Fantasies of unlimited power and money
- Fantasies of the perfect relationship
- Fantasies of a knight in shining armor coming for you
- Fantasies of rejecting the person who rejected you
- Excessive daydreaming
- Blame
- Resentment
- Rumination
- Saving or rescuing others
- Being saved or rescued
- Creating crisis situations

- Creating drama
- Seeing conspiracies or ill-intent everywhere
- Paranoia or fear of others
- Impulsive behavior
- Reckless behavior
- Changing careers
- Moving constantly
- Being a workaholic
- Other: _____

Next up, we want to look at the underlying bodily sensations. Circle any feelings that apply, and note where you experience them in the body.

BODY LOCATION:

- Head
- Throat
- Neck
- Shoulders
- Chest
- Heart
- Core
- Stomach
- Pelvis/Reproductive
- Legs
- Other: _____

SENSATIONS:

- Numb
- Empty
- Hole
- Void
- Blocked up
- Bored
- Tight
- Hollow
- Burning
- Pressure
- Squeezing
- Aching
- Constricted
- Weak
- Deadness
- Tired
- Black hole
- Missing
- Can't explain it
- Other: _____

Your homework: Look at the list of items you circled from "External Measures of Worth." Over the coming weeks and months, make a conscious effort to try "not doing" those things. If you make a mistake, don't worry about it. Just experiment with doing fewer and fewer of them. Instead, turn your attention to the internal bodily sensations noted on the previous pages.

The Perfectionist

There's nothing wrong with doing a good job, but perfectionism becomes more of an obsession than anything else. Perfectionists believe if they do everything right all the time, then they can finally be loved. This extends into careers, physical appearance, family life, and relationships. Ironically, they end up with the short end of the stick because in all of their hard work, they end up surrounded by people who really aren't holding up their end of the bargain.

Perfectionists may make a minor error in a relationship, and spend days or weeks berating themselves for it, fearful that they "ruined everything" and are now at a disadvantage in the relationship.

Perfectionists always keep busy with new projects and accomplishments. They are driven by a belief that if they just achieve this next big thing, *then* they'll feel good. So they spend time fantasizing about that thing, how great it will be when it's finished, and how much everyone will appreciate it. They do everything right, obsessively focused down to the last detail. But inevitably once that thing is successfully finished (and perfectionists successfully finish many projects), it is never enough. They may have a short burst of excitement or relief, especially leading up to the final steps of the accomplishment, but it doesn't last long. Sooner or later, they are drawn toward their next great accomplishment or idea. The protective self convinces them that this *next* thing will make them feel much better, and the past thing they just accomplished wasn't actually that big of a deal, and that's why they don't feel so great.

Perfectionists will introduce themselves to others as a humble list of their accomplishments, their GPA, and various other successes. They're not actually describing themselves, but rather a list of things they have done. No matter how big this list becomes, they never feel quite insulated or worthy enough, which means they need to keep adding to the list.

A perfectionist will work a million times harder than everyone else to prove that they are worthy, but even when they succeed at all of those things, there is a nagging voice inside of them that tells them it was all "too easy" or "not real"—that anyone could have done it—that they need to do something different, better, bigger, to prove themselves. They are unable to actually enjoy any of their own successes, despite having done far more than the average person.

If you are a perfectionist, the protective self will keep you on this hamster wheel of accomplishments until you finally realize that it's not working. No matter how many perfect projects you complete or milestones you exceed, it will never be enough. But only *you* can become aware of this fact and start to decline these exciting ideas from the protective self. It wants you to keep going so you *don't* slow down. It doesn't want you to experience what's going on in your body. It doesn't want you to spend any more time with that mean, nagging voice.

The Protective Self

Core Wound: Perfectionists are often dealing with an underlying sense of defectiveness ("something is wrong with me"). Imposter syndrome is common, with a fear that others might discover them as a fraud, despite not doing anything fraudulent.

Protective Self: The protective self that covers this wound is trying to prove the opposite. It is trying to prove that you are *not* defective, perhaps through accomplishments, being overly "nice" to everyone, social media validation, or perfecting appearance.

Dysfunctional Healing Approach: Healing can be really difficult at first, because perfectionists think they need to do everything "right" in order to heal. Approaching forgiveness or spirituality becomes more of a managed project, rather than a non-judgmental exploration of their own feelings. They criticize and judge themselves for making mistakes (and then judge themselves for being judgmental!). Perfectionists can eventually overcome this by learning to be more easygoing and humorous with the process. It's not about doing everything right. It's about accepting both the successes and the mistakes.

Conversation with Sarah

Sarah is incredibly accomplished and successful for her age. She is always taking on new projects (even outside of work) and looking to prove herself. At work, she volunteers to take the lead on everything because no one else can be trusted to do it right. All she needs is "one more" accomplishment to finally feel at peace. On dates, she often describes herself by describing her accomplishments and presenting her perfect life. But no matter how many people acknowledge her success, she feels a dull, numb sensation.

"Can you tell me more about the numb sensation?" I asked.

"It's sort of all over," said Sarah, motioning up and down her body. "It feels like everything is just disconnected and tired."

"Well, tired definitely makes sense," I said. "You've been really busy with work!"

"That's true," she said. "We actually just finished a huge project. My boss is so happy about it, so we're all going out to celebrate next week."

"Congratulations!" I said. "You must feel so proud."

"That's exactly the problem," she said. "I worked crazy hours to get this thing implemented perfectly. Poured my heart and soul into it. And now that it's over, I just feel numb again."

"Can you take some time to enjoy your accomplishment?" I asked. "Maybe a little vacation with your friends?"

"I can't." She laughed. "I already volunteered for our next project. It's going to be even bigger than the last one! We're revamping the entire way we do business. Plus, I offered to run my volleyball league this year, so I'll be swamped with that."

"That sounds like a really full schedule," I said. "Does it give you time to take care of yourself, or explore the numb feeling?"

"Well, I like to keep busy," she said. "And you know what's funny about the numbness?"

"What's that?"

"It actually feels a lot better when I'm working," she said. "Like it's still there, but it doesn't feel nearly as bad. I don't notice it as much. So maybe the solution is just to keep busy."

Sarah's homework: Stop taking on new projects. When you get the urge to accomplish something newer and bigger than ever before, to experience the surge of energy and excitement, just notice that and politely decline it. Notice when you are seeking approval from others by being extremely kind or generous. Instead, sit with the feeling of numbness.

The Cluster-B Abuse Survivor

People coming out of cluster-B relationships (with sociopaths, narcissists, borderline or histrionic personalities) carry a misery about them that no one else seems to understand. The standard breakup advice of "time heals all wounds" or "just get over it" doesn't seem to apply. Instead, it's like they've been disconnected from the things that make life worth living. Their natural joy and love has disappeared, replaced by constant anxiety and self-doubt.

These relationships start out better than anything you've ever experienced. The disordered individual seems to love and need you more than any partner you've known. They latch on, mimicking your hopes and dreams, even mirroring your vocal and texting mannerisms. Of course, you don't know this is happening, because you don't know what cluster-B disorders are (yet). You're just freely falling in love, grateful to have found this amazing "soul mate."

But inevitably, things take a turn for the worse. This person becomes controlling, manipulative, critical, dismissive, and unfaithful. They do hurtful things and then blame you for reacting. You desperately keep trying to re-create the original perfect dynamic, wondering where in the world that person went. You are punished with the silent treatment and other painful behaviors. Every time you're feeling ready to leave, your partner swoops back in with promises that remind you of the person they used to be.

In relationships with borderlines, you find they're having a new crisis or meltdown on a near-regular basis. Every time you thought you solved one issue, they have a different one. You used to feel special for helping them, but now it seems they're just using you as a sounding board for their never-ending problems. And their problems seem to have such trivial, simple solutions. But they reject and ignore these solutions, almost as if they prefer being victims of a stressful and dramatic life. You were taught to validate and sympathize, but this often seems to enable unhealthy and impulsive decisions in your partner. For example, they may come home sobbing and ranting about their abusive boss or their slavelike work conditions. You know these are massive exaggerations, and if you validate them, then your partner may use it as ammo to quit their job.

In relationships with narcissists and sociopaths, their initial obsession with you starts to dwindle and you find they're waving other people in your face. Nothing you seem to do is good enough for them, and they're constantly seeking attention and adoration from anyone who will give it to them. This causes you to become more frantic and unstable as you desperately try to restore your "perfect" relationship.

Eventually, things end badly. They cheat on you and replace you with someone else in a matter of weeks, showering someone new with all of the attention they originally gave you. Or you leave them, so they stalk and harass you to give themselves some sense of power over you.

Either way, your body and mind are in shock. You have no idea what just happened. You went from a euphoric high to a devastating low, wondering if you've lost the best thing that ever happened to you, despite knowing that this person mistreated you constantly.

These experiences create a great deal of cognitive dissonance, which is what typically inspires you to start searching for answers and validation. Once you come across the description of cluster-B personality disorders, suddenly everything clicks. There are words and patterns to describe the chaos you just experienced. You share your story, read experiences from others, and finally have some understanding of what happened.

But the problem is, none of this seems to actually make you

feel whole again. You find yourself wondering what happened to your "old self": the cheerful, loving person who laughed and smiled with others. Instead, you feel disconnected, anxious, and on edge. You obsess and ruminate about every little detail of the relationship. Time doesn't heal all wounds, and instead you find yourself feeling more isolated and detached from the world around you.

Feeling that your original identity was broken by this encounter, you may be trying to rebuild it from scratch. Taking personality quizzes, learning about empaths and "highly sensitive people," taking pride in your ability to sense emotions in others—these things may sound good because they are the "opposite" of a narcissist, but they're actually quite unhealthy for you and others. We are not meant to be hyperaware of the moods of people around us.

This makes it extremely difficult to enjoy anyone's company, when we're always on the lookout for shifts in their feelings. This is a coping mechanism we learned so that we could prevent or predict certain outcomes from the disordered individual: rejection, silence, and anger. The problem with healthy relationships is that our sensors can be incorrect. We're not meant to spend our time obsessing over what everyone else is thinking or feeling. All of this external focus makes it hard to figure out what's going on inside ourselves.

No matter how hard you might work to rebuild yourself after a cluster-B relationship, your new identity likely feels shaky. Something still feels wrong. Something inside of you feels broken, and you don't know how to repair it.

The Protective Self

Core Wound: Pretty much every survivor I encounter who explores the cluster-B disorders is dealing with a *deep sense of rejection and/or inadequacy*. While they may feel bursts of self-worth and pride by labeling disordered behavior for what it is, or having their story validated by others, none of this actually resolves the underlying rejection wound. Having been cheated on and replaced, and often publicly humiliated, these survivors tend to feel inferior and unwanted ("I am not enough. Others are better than me"). There is also often a fear of being crazy, and a nagging doubt that everything was secretly their own fault.

Protective Self: The protective self that covers this wound is trying to prove the opposite. It is trying to prove that you are *not* inferior, perhaps through accomplishing things, taking care of others, playing therapist, or analyzing and diagnosing people. Instead of *feeling* the rejection, it *thinks* about the betrayal. Cluster-B abuse survivors tend to become hyperfocused on others, because their own internal world is damaged. They ruminate about their experiences and carry (understandable) resentment about the injustice that occurred. They may also try to find worth in identities that are the "opposite" of their abuser: "My abuser was a psychopath, but

I am an empath" or "My abuser was borderline, but I am extremely reasonable and logical." Depending on the severity of the wounding, this protective self can be very difficult to penetrate because it is positively convinced that it is completely fine, driven by a sort of manic and combative resentment that is completely focused on diagnosing or exposing the abuser, and unable to slow down for introspection. It may completely deny the possibility of feeling rejected, because "they are disordered and they can't feel love, so I'm glad we broke up."

Dysfunctional Healing Approach: This protective self tends to approach healing by focusing on the "other." The internal gauge is broken, so healing is all about other people. Forgiveness becomes all about analyzing or understanding the perpetrator (when it's really just an *internal* process of letting go). This protective self also seeks a great deal of validation from others, when it's more a matter of building a private relationship with the feelings in your own body.

It's Not About You

My first book was about the patterns and behaviors of cluster-B folks in relationships. This book isn't asking you to forget about any of that, but rather to turn your focus inward. Because the truth is, what happened had very little to do with you, so what good can come from focusing on this past relationship anymore?

This is one of the hardest things for survivors to understand, but it's also really important. Cluster-B disordered individuals are often called "energy vampires" because they drain their targets of all natural love, joy, and sanity. Cluster-B personalities are unknowingly lost on a never-ending quest to fill an internal void (often referred to as boredom, emptiness, unfeelable emotions, the rejected self).

Similar to an addict, they believe that external factors will fill that void, so they are constantly looking outward for attention and adoration. This also explains the delusions of grandeur, as their disorder convinces them that unlimited power or fame or money or the "perfect" relationship will finally fill that void.

This false self is always seeking external validation, blaming outwardly when the void is inevitably not filled. Like a black hole, they will suck the energy out of you until you have nothing left to offer, then discard you and blame you because the void is still there. The narrative of "you" will always change depending on how they feel.

With time, you must come to understand that this cycle had nothing to do with you. You were neither the "perfect savior" from the idealization period, nor the "crazy" partner from the devaluation period. You were seen as a solution to their void, you were put on a pedestal, you failed to fill the void (no external factor can), so you were devalued and cast aside.

As you begin to understand the sheer magnitude of psychological damage required to cause such disordered thinking, you realize that no amount of your love (or anyone else's) can fill their void, because it is a void centered around a protective self.

They never attached to you, despite all of their sweeping words, which is why they try to intensely manufacture all the normal feelings of love and bonding, and it's also why they are able to detach and do the same thing to someone else in one day.

Cluster-B disordered individuals are incapable of attaching to other human beings, so they hone all of these other skills such as seduction, flattery, mirroring—all in an attempt to mimic what they see other people doing: loving each other. The problem is, they see "love" as receiving constant attention and adoration. This is what they give to you, and this is what they want to receive in return.

Imagine a dog who wants to be a cat, running around and trying to get everyone to tell him he's a cat. When they tell him he's a cat, he feels validated as a cat. He praises and rewards the people who call him a cat, grooming them to keep calling him a cat. But no matter how many people tell him he's a cat, he still looks in the mirror and sees a dog. He hates the dog. He cannot love the dog. He wants to be a cat. He blames everyone else for failing to convince him he's a cat, and finds another one hundred people to tell him he's a cat.

Do you see that no amount of your love or validation or sympathy will fix this issue?

You also start to see that none of these things had anything to do with you or your worth, but rather the repeated cycle of someone unknowingly living out their own personal hell, over and over again. Part of this hell is that it literally locks them into this false reality, convincing them they are superior, and dismissing or ridiculing actual emotions.

In the process, they leave voids in others, feelings of deep worthlessness, rejection, shame, and inadequacy. All of this might be locked away as numbness for a while (PTSD).

You can break this cycle by meeting your own internal pain with self-love and a heartfelt understanding that this experience truly was not your fault. Whatever happened to them to cause this disorder was likely not their fault either, but now you see that your love cannot possibly break that psychological barrier. Your first priority is to turn your focus *inward*, allowing yourself to feel the emotions you were told were wrong.

They mirror your hopes and dreams because they don't have an identity of their own, so they're always trying to find it in others. They'll get manically obsessed and hyperfocused on their latest target because this person is the solution to their constant emptiness and boredom.

Except the problem is internal, so inevitably they still feel bad no matter how well you treat them, so they punish you and find someone else and devalue everything about you.

When you understand the extent of the psychological damage required to cause these disorders, you will stop trying to analyze your relationship and wonder if it could have worked out if you had done X or if they had done Y. You never met the "real" them because *they* don't know the real them. Their brains and bodies have done psychological gymnastics to keep them out.

You'll also start to realize this entire process had *nothing* to do with you. It would honestly be selfish to try to get back together with them, because you're basically asking a mentally ill person to resume copying your personality, when they should instead be going through years of intensive therapy to work on finding their true self. And even if they found their true self, that person will probably be nothing like the person you met. You might not even like them at all.

And so the most important thing you can do is release the messages they left behind (not enough, worthless, bad, inadequate) and learn how to love yourself. Otherwise you'll just keep searching for this instant perfect connection with someone else to "complete" you and find yourself right back in the same nightmare.

Many survivors doubt themselves, repeatedly seeking external validation at the beginning of the healing process. This is common and understandable. But ultimately we must build the tools needed to carry this pain and nurture ourselves back to health. Therapy can help us to develop these techniques, but we are the only ones who can dedicate ourselves to daily practice and free our hearts from the false prison passed on to us.

We cannot search outwardly for peace, any more than the dog who wants to be a cat.

But Why Did They Hurt Me?

One of the most common patterns among the cluster-B disorders is an obsessive need to know if they hurt you. Negative emotional reactions are deemed a "success," and they especially want to know if you still want them even after they have mistreated you.

They will intentionally wave new partners or exes in your face to see if you'll react. They invent pointless reasons to contact you, just to see if they can get a reaction out of you. If they don't get a reaction, they continue escalating and prodding until they do.

To people with cluster-B disorders, it's very important that you still like them, even if they don't like you. They want to be 100 percent sure they are the one to reject you, and never the other way around. These "victories" give them bursts of self-worth and excitement, but of course this is a pretty hollow form of self-worth.

Oftentimes, survivors get sucked into this "game" and wish they had been the one to reject first, so they could "win." But this completely flies in the face of healthy vulnerability and attachment in romantic relationships. When people view relationships and rejection as a game, they have already lost. Love is not about making sure other people want/love/adore/need/miss you. That is a false, ego-based concept of love.

Your attention provides the personality disordered individual with a burst of prideful energy that keeps their false self afloat. This is why they need you to adore them in the idealization, it's why they are constantly trying to get reactions out of you when you're together, and it's why they need to know you still care after the breakup.

Your praise, reactions, adoration, and even hatred are all proof that they exist. That they are important. That they matter. Look how strongly you reacted, they must have been important! Without any internal compass of their own, they rely on external measures of worth to prove their value.

But the protective self is never satisfied. It's like trying to fill a black hole, an infinite void. Even after a "victory," their nagging boredom or emptiness comes creeping back. But instead of trying to explore that uncomfortable sensation, they quickly find a new target to distract themselves and keep the protective self alive.

The protective self is never satisfied.

By understanding this, we can let go of the win/lose mentality that often comes with cluster-B relationships. Just because someone claims victory doesn't mean there was a game worth playing. So often, we get stuck in this rut of trying to prove who cares the least, who moved on the fastest, but again this is all based on "not letting them win." It's a waste of our time.

Our greatest victory comes from exploring our own uncomfortable sensations that arise from rejection. When a trusted loved one rejects us in an abrupt way, we often absorb very difficult messages. Especially if we were immediately replaced or compared with others, it's common for feelings of inadequacy and worthlessness to form.

If we can explore these difficult sensations (rather than numbing them out), we can build a kind relationship with ourselves and eventually free our hearts. As we begin to understand why people with cluster-B disorders reject others, it becomes much easier to understand and release our own underlying feelings of rejection.

It is sort of like a wound being passed around, and the amazing thing is, we all have the ability to slow down with our external distractions, sit with the inner discomfort until it reveals the wound, and realize: "Hey, this isn't even true. It's not who I am."

Once again, you are starting to realize that the other person's behavior has very little to do with you, and you can simply let the rejected feelings go.

What If They're Not Cluster B?

One of the most common questions asked during recovery is: "Was he or she really a sociopath? What if I'm just saying that to feel better about myself?" Survivors ask this question over and over again, because for most of us, the alternative is the cluster B's reality: "You are crazy, jealous, sensitive, paranoid, unattractive, unwanted." And so we oscillate back and forth between these two realities: bad other, or bad self.

While I believe that education about the cluster Bs are essential to healing and sanity restoration (especially in the early stages as we break the chemical bond and learn to go No Contact), we eventually must learn to release this duality.

In a way, our own sense of self hinges on someone else being bad. This is not sustainable, and it slowly leads to some strange personality changes where you might find yourself frequently analyzing and judging others (and yourself), constantly frustrated that people aren't behaving the way they are "supposed to" (including yourself).

Underneath it all is still that same nagging voice: "What if it was all me? What if it's my fault?"—that voice only fuels more of the same behaviors. That's the voice we want to get in touch with—the one the protective self tries to avoid by trying harder and harder to accomplish, be nice, and prove you are good.

If you attempt forgiveness, there's a strong chance you'll end up feeling like you've been teleported back in time: cognitive dissonance, self-doubt, wondering if you should reach out to your abuser. Without your security blanket of "bad other," you are stuck with "bad self" again. The thing is, this sense of "bad self" lives in the body, regardless of whether or not your ex was "bad other." So if blaming the bad other won't fix this, what will?

As we begin to fully open to our pain and fears, there seems to be an equally proportionate amount of love that starts to develop to hold it all. It can feel completely overwhelming at first, and it might take a long time, but I promise this love appears when you realize you are suffering. We can't do this when we are stuck in external ruminations and resentments.

This love is not ego-driven and has absolutely nothing to do with being good or bad, right or wrong. It has nothing to do with the past. It simply sees you as a human being suffering, in need of love and kindness. There is no longer anything to prove.

In this process, we are not asking ourselves to pretend it "wasn't that bad." We're asking ourselves to acknowledge and embrace the full pain of rejection, abandonment, and abuse. We're asking ourselves to replace old messages of "not enough" with new messages of love and kindness.

Many survivors do uncharacteristic things during and after the relationship, including betrayals of their own values and morals. Again, anyone is bound to do crazy things when they encounter one of these relationships. But the word "sociopath" or "borderline" won't erase that shame. Sure, it helps you rationalize your behavior, but it doesn't let go of that heartfelt sense of "I am bad." Only unconditional love will do that.

The question "What if they're not really cluster B?" loses all its significance when we come to love ourselves regardless of the answer. In the past, we might have feared that without our security blanket, "maybe they were actually perfect" or "I'll end up going back to them." But in the end, meeting all of that with love simply erases those fears. The healthy, pure love that we find from this journey naturally guides us toward the same authenticity in others.

But We Were So in Love

The "love" that cluster-B disordered individuals want is a lot like the drug an addict wants. It's not really love, but a constant source of external validation, reassurance, and attention.

Similar to an addict, they manipulate others to get their fix. And when they don't get their fix, they're bored and empty, because they're stuck with their own void. And even when they *do* get their fix, they're abusive and manipulative because their internal problem cannot be solved by external solutions.

Addicts eventually learn that *they* are the ones who must change, not the rest of the world. In order to stop harming others, they must sit with that unbearable void and spend a great deal of time healing it, rather than trying to fill it with drugs. Just like an addict, the only hope for those with a cluster-B disorder is when they decide *they* are the ones who must change, not the rest of the world (please: no more "guides" on how to be in a relationship with them and cater to their needs). They need to sit with that unbearable void and spend years healing it. That's the only solution.

"All I want is love" sounds much cuter than "All I want is heroin," but when it comes to cluster-B disorders, it's the same thing.

The love they want is not really love. It's a constant, guaranteed source of adoration and attention. Validation of their identity and worth. Confirmation that they are lovable, that they can do anything and you'll never leave. Manic and obsessive, romanticizing others as the solution to everything. Constantly reassured that they are sexy and beautiful and needed.

The protective self is insatiable, like a black hole. It can never be "loved" enough because it is not real.

This is not love. It's obsession and infatuation, a subconscious belief that you will cure their void of emptiness. Hence the devaluation when they still feel bad no matter how much love you gave them.

Here are some qualities of love rooted in narcissism:

- You are perfect
- You are flawless
- You are beautiful, sexy, the hottest person in the world

- Constant communication is good
- Adoration, praise, attention are good
- Negative emotions are unacceptable
- Consumes your entire life and thoughts
- Frantic and intense
- Addictive

This is a lot of ego stuff. It *feels* really good at first, like all their attention is laser-focused on you and you're the most important person in the world. It's intense, they're in your thoughts all the time, they make you feel special and unique. Everything you do is perfect (at first). And when they leave, you worry you'll never find that feeling again.

But what if that feeling wasn't even love? I mean, of course you were in love. But what if there was a much more powerful kind of love that you had yet to discover? One that made the above type of love look like complete nonsense (because it is).

I think Yogi Berra said, "You don't know what you don't know," and that's exactly the problem here. We're not going to look for another type of love if we don't even know it exists, or how it feels. So it's easy to get stuck with this false blueprint of love and develop all sorts of maladaptive needs based on that. Suddenly we're looking outward for love, imagining a savior, or saving others, stuck with vengeful thoughts, seeking external validation and approval, trying to do everything perfectly.

In order to find a different kind of love, we need to tame our own ego that has been hugely inflated, criticized, and ultimately betrayed. Underneath all of that is where you'll find the good stuff: feelings, the heart, the real you.

As your buried feelings come out, they're likely to be pretty unpleasant: inadequacy, anger, jealousy, rejection, self-doubt, shame. Instead of turning away from these difficult feelings, we need to welcome them with open arms. This won't be easy at first because your brain is used to thinking in a certain way, but you can rewire it with new habits and daily practice. Every time you try non-judgmentally to allow a feeling to exist (instead of analyzing it to death), it will melt a bit more, like an ice cube, and eventually wash away.

The more we do this, the more our blueprint changes. As we work through the feelings, we find a softer place in our heart. We cannot think our way into this place. We cannot find it in anyone else, only ourselves. When your own feelings (even painful ones) are at home in your heart, you'll probably start to feel bursts of joy and gratitude. Relief, like you can breathe again. This is when we start to discover another type of love:

- Freeing
- Joyful
- Grateful
- Spiritual growth
- Forgiving
- Open to flaws
- Calming
- All emotions are welcome
- Independent

- Kind and humorous
- Patient
- Infinite

We feel it for ourselves first, then we can offer it freely to others. Through this self-nurturing process, we slowly discover what real love feels like (not rescuing and sympathy and flattery and attention). You will never again be interested in the "love" that is found in cluster-B relationships.

Conversation with Mel

Several months ago, Mel was dumped by a narcissistic man. In the beginning of their relationship, everything was perfect. He showered her with attention and praise, consumed her entire life. He spoke of marriage and children. But it turned out he was playing this game with another woman at the same time. He eventually replaced Mel with this woman. Now Mel cannot stop checking his Facebook page to see updates about his new relationship. She's looking for proof that their relationship will fail too. Nearly all of her focus is spent learning about his mental disorder. He can't feel love, and she can, so she wins. She takes on new identities as an "empath" and a "highly sensitive person," determined to prove herself as the opposite of him. By playing detective and exposing him as a fraud, she's distracted from this newfound void inside of her—the part of her that he *stole*.

"What does the void feel like in your body?" I asked.

"I don't know," she said distantly. "It's just like there's nothing where my emotions and love used to be. It's like my old self went away."

"That sounds so difficult," I said. "What are you doing to explore that sensation?"

"Well, I've joined a lot of online communities for people recovering from narcissistic abuse. That's been really helpful." Then she smiles. "Of course, you already know that, because you run one."

I laughed. "I guess I have a little bit of experience. What sort of stuff do you talk about on the website?"

"Well, I tell my story and read the stories of other survivors," she said. "It's so great to meet others who have been through the same thing, you know? Helps you realize you're not alone."

"That's great," I said. "Are the stories helping you heal?"

"I think so," she said. "I just wish he'd break up with the new girlfriend. Then I'd know I'm not crazy, and I'd be able to move on. I seriously want to send her a warning message so she knows what she's getting into. They look so happy on Facebook, but it can't possibly last."

"You're still checking his Facebook page?"

"I can't stop!" she said. "It's like some sort of obsession. But I've decided to go No Contact, so I'll be counting the days on my calendar to keep me on track."

"Do your online friends help you stay No Contact?"

"Oh, yeah," she said. "They're amazing. A lot of beautiful and sensitive souls. I'm learning so much from them. I'm realizing I'm an empath, and I took a personality test that said I'm an INFJ, which is the most sensitive and empathetic of all the types. Makes sense that I ended up with a psychopath!"

"What do you mean?"

"Well, we're opposites, right?" she said. "Psychopaths can't feel love and emotions. Those things are like my superpowers, and he was trying to destroy them because he was jealous of me."

"Got it," I said. "As you learn more about your empathetic qualities, and about psychopathy, does that help to heal the void we talked about earlier?"

"Hmm, I'm not sure." She paused. "I mean, the void feeling is still there, but it's a lot less noticeable when I focus on that other stuff. Honestly, I think it'll go away once his new relationship falls apart. I just need to know for sure that he's not capable of love, then I'll feel completely better."

Mel's homework: Stop checking his Facebook page and comparing yourself to the new relationship. Sit instead with the "void" feeling. Do not try to analyze the void or form a story around it. Just stay with the feeling, exactly as it is. If other uncomfortable sensations start to arise, be prepared to welcome these with a friendly curiosity.

Conversation with Elliot

When Elliot first met his girlfriend, he thought he'd found the woman of his dreams. Amy was loving, nurturing, and seemed to be his soul mate. They had everything in common—the same hopes, dreams, and insecurities. Amy quickly revealed a history of abusive partners and a traumatic childhood, all of which tugged at Elliot's heartstrings. He promised to be different, to never hurt her the way the others did. But as their relationship progressed, Amy began accusing him of things he didn't do—objectifying her, using her, even cheating on her. Before long, he found that he had become her latest "abusive" partner. The more time that passed, the more he began to fear that he actually was an abuser. No matter how hard he tried to prove himself, to save and help her, it never seemed to be enough.

"She had another episode today," said Elliot.

"I'm sorry to hear that. What happened?"

"Nothing!" he said, exasperated. "Literally nothing. I asked her to take out the trash on her way to work. She said she was too busy, so I told her it was no problem and said I would do it. Then she accused me of 'taking a tone with her' and within a minute she was yelling that I don't appreciate her, and that I was manipulating the situation to seem like the hero."

"That sounds exhausting," I said.

"She's so freaking dramatic. Everything goes from zero to a hundred with no warning. Sobbing and screaming about nothing. Then she accuses *me* of yelling at *her* when I'm speaking calmly! Why does every trivial thing have to be automatically escalated to trauma and abuse?"

"Because she is most comfortable in the victim role," I said. "By painting you as a perpetrator, she is able to remain the victim and avoid exploring her own uncomfortable feelings of shame."

"I just don't get it," he said. "No matter what I do, no matter how calm or nice I am, it makes no difference. She still reacts this way over nothing."

"Right, because it has nothing to do with you."

"But in the beginning, she seemed so happy with me. If I could just get us back to that place, then everything would be perfect again."

"That person wasn't really her, though," I said. "That was her version of who she thought you wanted her to be, so she could become your perfect non-abandonable partner."

"Some of it was definitely real, though," Elliot said. "And if I could just get her to remember that, I think we could get somewhere."

"She doesn't seem like she wants to get somewhere, though," I said. "It seems like every attempt at help is interpreted as a threat or power play. You can't help someone who is stuck in a trance like that. They need to want to get help themselves."

"She wants help sometimes," he said. "She breaks down sobbing sometimes in shame, admitting the hurtful things she's done. She's so remorseful. She doesn't want to be like that."

"Does she stop doing the hurtful things?"

Elliot paused. "No."

"So even if her intentions are good in the moment, she's unable to follow through with her promises. That doesn't seem fair to you."

"I know, but she needs me. Seriously, she will harm herself if I don't take care of her. I'm all she has."

"That's not a healthy position for you to be in, though," I said. "You are her partner, not her therapist."

He laughed. "Well, we're way beyond that point. She gave me a few articles about how I can help her feel safe and loved, with validation and sympathy."

"Do you want to be in a relationship that requires you to follow a guide?"

"I want to do whatever it takes to fix things and go back to the way it was," he said. "So if validating can help her, then isn't it worth a try?"

"People with borderline personality disorder are constantly searching for external causes and solutions to their problems. You could be the most perfect, loving, supportive boyfriend in the world—but eventually she would have another outburst. Because her problem is internal, not external. She can keep trying to pad the entire world, but it will never be enough."

"So what am I supposed to do? And don't tell me to 'run,' like all the other stigmatizing resources out there."

"You're spending all this time thinking about her. Her problems, her past, her moods—trying to modify your own behavior to change *her* behavior. That's a lot of focus on someone else. I'm curious, what do *you* feel like?"

"I am sick of trying so hard, and having her do the same thing over and over again—that's how I feel."

"That's still about her, though," I said. "How do *you* feel? Like in your body."

"I don't know anymore." He sighed. "Honestly, I don't have time to think about myself anymore. Her problems are always so much more dramatic and important than mine."

"That's not true," I said. "Your feelings are equally as important, you just aren't forcing them upon other people."

"There's some part of me that feels like I can't express those feelings," he said. "Figures I ended up with someone who expresses enough for the both of us."

"Well, what would happen if you expressed your true feelings? What would they be?"

"I don't know," he said. "It just feels like a big ball of dread and numbness. It's honestly easier to focus on her problems."

Elliot's homework: Stop focusing so much on your partner and begin expending some of that same energy on your own feelings. Don't spend so much time analyzing the behaviors of someone whose behavior has nothing to do with you. Instead, explore the ball of dread and numbness in your own body.

Codependent

*Instead of seeing other people's dissatisfaction as an issue
for them to resolve on their own, I internalized it and
interpreted it to mean I wasn't good enough.*

—ILENE S. COHEN, *WHEN IT'S* NEVER *ABOUT YOU*

Codependents are some of my favorite people to work with, because they tend to be the most caring and compassionate people on the planet. Codependents spend a lot of time taking care of others: thinking about their problems, anticipating their needs, and avoiding potential problems by trying to do everything right.

Codependents are the type of people to notice at dinner when two mutual friends are growing irritable with each other, or a sensitive topic is being approached, or someone's feelings are being hurt (by someone who is not the codependent). And then the codependent will try to improve—or avoid—the situation with diplomacy, humor, or whatever else fits the situation.

Those don't necessarily sound like negative qualities! The problem is, that same kindness they extend to others is not offered inward. Codependents are often *so awful* to themselves. They doubt their intuition, blame themselves when other people misbehave, and worry that they're being too harsh when they stand up for themselves. In relationships, they tend to put up with being mistreated for far longer than most would stick around. They try to stay and fix things, worried that they're not being flexible enough. They feel crazy or bad for having needs, and even worse for asserting those needs. In their careers, they probably work harder than most people and accomplish an incredible amount, but then come back to a voice that says, "You're just faking, you're a fraud, it was easy, anyone could have done that."

> **Codependents feel responsible for *everything*.**

Even reading this section, a codependent might think, "Hey, I resonate with that," and then another mean voice takes over and says, "You're just saying that to avoid taking responsibility. You know it's secretly your fault." And that's the voice that drives it all. Because codependents feel responsible for *everything*. From group projects, to relationship communication, to the emotions of others, the codependent can never relax.

And even when they do everything right, it's *never enough*.

Never enough.

Never enough.

Until they take the necessary steps to recover, alcoholics continue to drink, addicts continue to use substances, borderlines continue to cause crisis and chaos, narcissists continue to manipulate and seek attention. No amount of effort or love from codependents can solve these issues, and yet, for some reason they continue to pour their valuable resources into these projects that are doomed from the start. They find that their once-tough boundaries have crumbled, and they are once again excusing behavior they swore they'd never put up with.

They are happy with the little things, forgiving and flexible with everyone in their life. And yet, they will find that the people surrounding them seem to find complaints with everything they do. Their partner can say and do unacceptable things on a daily basis, which the codependent will try to explain and understand ("they had a difficult childhood!"). But the moment codependents make a single mistake, they berate themselves for it, obsess over it, and wonder if they're crazy. For this reason, they come up short in relationships, over and over again. Because they're unable to recognize that the balance is skewed, and unable to recognize that they're not getting what they deserve from a healthy relationship. Their self-doubt keeps things forever skewed in their partner's favor.

Even relationships with non-disordered individuals are

destined to have conflicts and challenges. It is not the codependent's job to control or avoid those things. This is an exhausting task, and it'll eventually result in depression and resentment. When you spend so much time thinking about other people, you inevitably become frustrated because your expectations are so often broken. You are in direct conflict with reality, thinking people *should* behave a certain way, but missing the much more obvious point that they are *not* behaving that way.

Codependents place a great deal of importance on the reactions of other people to define their own self-worth. They are constantly assessing situations, feeling good when others react well and feeling ashamed when others react negatively. They can go through most of their lives feeling pretty good about themselves if everything is going perfectly and everyone is happy with them. But life has an interesting way of presenting toxic relationships to codependents, which is when everything starts to become unraveled.

The codependent's unbalanced relationship patterns eventually lead to serious emotional issues, which they may continue to ignore until it becomes so serious that they begin to manifest symptoms of C-PTSD—hypervigilance, revenge fantasies, mood swings, and isolation. This severe discomfort may feel unfair and wrong, but it's actually a blessing in disguise. It's the first motivator for codependents to begin paying attention to what's going on in their own bodies, which is a first step toward caring about their own needs and emotions.

Codependents might actually be reluctant to resonate with this protective self, because they assume there must be something far more sinister about themselves. It would not be uncommon for codependents to read this book and fear they have borderline personality disorder, despite acting nothing like the diagnostic criteria. Codependents will have relationships with psychopaths and then spend months worrying that *they* might be the psychopath, failing to realize that their incessant guilt and fear is living proof that they're not psychopaths.

Codependents tend to feel a tremendous amount of self-doubt any time they think negatively about someone else, but the moment someone suggests something negative about them, they will entertain it for all eternity. They worry that it might be true, even if it has absolutely no bearing in reality. This is not a happy way to exist.

The Protective Self

Core Wound: Many codependents are dealing with a sense of worthlessness and "not enough," afraid that they could be rejected and abandoned. This may have come from childhood issues or a traumatic relationship that taught them to focus on the needs of others. High-conflict families can also teach codependents how to navigate other people's feelings in order to avoid discomfort. Especially if a parent is prone to outbursts and rigid rules, children can learn at a young age not to express their needs in order to keep the peace. Codependents tend to carry a huge sense of over-responsibility for others, and deep down believe that everything is their fault.

Protective Self: The protective self that covers this wound is trying to prove the opposite. It is trying to prove that you *are* enough—that you have worth—usually by taking care of people in need and taking on their problems as your own. The protective self takes pride in being compassionate to everyone, offering second (or third or fourth) chances where they are not warranted. It mistakes pity for love, and finds itself constantly drawn toward people who are emotionally unavailable and drain the energy from them. It thinks if it "helps" or "saves" people, they will eventually grow appreciative and give them the love they crave.

Dysfunctional Healing Approach: If you are codependent, your life is all about other people, and your approach to healing is often no different. You will focus on the people who wronged you, thinking forgiveness is about sympathizing with toxic people and allowing them back into your life. You may fantasize about beautiful tear-filled reconciliations, thinking you need to trust everyone in the world in order to heal, and then return to resentment when that inevitably backfires. You will try to "be good" and "do good," thinking if you are "good enough," then you will eventually be worthy of love. This type of "healing" can exacerbate and magnify the codependent's condition, as they try to be even *more* selfless and flexible and giving.

People Pleasing Doesn't Work

Codependency, caretaking, and people pleasing are all focused on the needs of others. Here are some of the common forms that people pleasing takes:

- Focused on the needs of others: Codependents tend to have a heightened awareness of the emotions of others. I don't mean "empath" or anything like that. They're just always aware of the moods and feelings around them.

- Conflict avoidant: They notice potential conflicts and douse the flames before things get a chance to blow up. They recognize when others are getting upset and do everything they can to prevent that from happening. They rehearse conversations in their mind and learn how to phrase things to elicit the most peaceful reaction.

- Guilt: They tend to feel guilty about way too much, even things that don't warrant guilt. They feel especially guilty when standing up for their own needs. They are quick to apologize and take the blame, even when they aren't at fault.

- Self-doubt: They often doubt their own feelings and intuition, especially if those things are "negative." For example, if someone else harms them and they try to set a boundary, they will spend days or weeks wondering if they were too harsh or secretly at fault.

· Perfectionistic: They tend to feel like they need to do everything "perfectly." If they make one mistake, they worry they've "ruined everything."

· Low self-worth: Rely heavily upon external validation and approval in order to feel "good enough." Can be immensely happy when everyone approves of them, but also immensely unhappy when others are upset with them.

Where do people-pleasing habits come from?

I'm not a therapist, and you're better off talking about this with a professional. But people pleasers often come from *high-conflict households*. It doesn't have to be abusive or cluster B by any means, just someone whose needs consistently overshadowed your own. Some examples:

· A parent who always had to argue and be right, so the people pleaser learns to sacrifice their own opinions in order to keep the peace
· A parent with anger issues, so the people pleaser learns to anticipate bad moods and calm them before it escalates to rage

- A parent with addiction or alcoholism issues, so the people pleaser learns to manage another person's illness
- A parent with borderline personality, so the people pleaser learns to soothe and comfort inappropriate dramatic crises and pity stories
- A parent with control issues and rigid rules, so the people pleaser learns to just do what they want to avoid unpleasant reactions
- A parent with depression or anxiety, so the people pleaser feels sorry for them and responsible for always being happy and cheering them up
- Parents who fight all the time, so the people pleaser learns to detect an argument brewing and rushes to quell things before a fight ensues
- One final, and very common, trigger for people pleasing is a cluster-B relationship. When you enter a relationship where everything is all about the other person, your focus may remain stuck externally.

The underlying theme is this: people pleasers feel personally responsible for the mental and emotional well-being of others. They may readily identify with examples in the above list and then feel deeply guilty for thinking that. This is because the above dynamics formed an unhealthy and anxious self-relationship, with inner conversations that go in circles forever:

"What if it's my fault? What if I haven't done enough? What

if I'm being unfair and not seeing things from the other perspective? Can I really trust my judgment?"

Whereas healthy parental dynamics instill a much calmer and quieter inner conversation:

"My choices and feelings are okay. I am loved even if I make a mistake. I am fine the way I am."

Shifting the conversation is doable. Believing it is the hard part. People pleasers are often very resistant to the idea of being unconditionally loved as they are (without having to *do* anything). Mindfulness can help explore these resistances and where they live in the body, so that they can be released.

How does this play into cluster-B relationships?

The combination actually makes a lot of sense. On one hand, you have a person who is completely focused on their own needs (cluster-B disorders). On the other, you have a person who is completely focused on the needs of others (people pleasers). If you imagine human beings as magnets, you can see why these two types would pull together.

During the honeymoon phase, it's a match made in heaven. Narcissists get their needs met, receiving constant adoration and praise. People pleasers feel fulfilled, finally appreciated and valued for their caretaking efforts. Narcissists essentially quell the anxious inner voice of the people pleaser by constantly offering approval and validation.

Of course this inevitably goes sour when narcissists become increasingly selfish, insensitive, and hostile. People pleasers implode, blaming themselves and trying even harder, despite their partner doing the opposite.

So the narcissist can say something as simple as "it's all about you" or "you're so selfish," and the people pleaser will immediately add this to their growing list of self-doubts instead of recognizing the blatant projection going on.

People pleasers' boundaries are shaky at best, afraid that standing up for themselves could end the entire relationship. They also worry about hurting their partner's feelings, despite mounting evidence that this is not a mutual concern.

So how can people pleasers protect themselves?

All this focus on others leads to a much more significant issue: no focus on the self.

This issue extends far beyond toxic relationships, and into toxic relationship recovery too. I spent so long focused on the red flags and warning signs, obsessing and ruminating about the misbehavior of others, I didn't even notice I was still completely distracted from my own issues.

As we turn our attention inward, we're likely to find a lot of stuff that needs our attention: low self-worth, fears, anxieties, feelings of rejection or inadequacy. By staying with these uncomfortable sensations, we learn how to build healthy relationships with ourselves, which naturally reflects in our relationships with others.

Red flags are important, but if we don't work on ourselves, we'll just continue doubting and guilting ourselves when we encounter red flags, which means we're not protected at all.

People pleasers often have no idea what they want, what their needs are, or what their boundaries look like. Everything is just about making sure others are happy. They can view any issue from another person's perspective, making excuses for others while offering themselves none of the same flexibility.

Cluster-B relationships are often the ultimate wake-up call that this does not work, making people pleasers' inner world so uncomfortable and painful that they are finally forced to pay attention to it.

Despite what you may have learned, it's not your job to manage the emotions of others. It's an exhausting role that may offer temporary bursts of self-worth, but ultimately will drain the life out of you. As we learn that we're responsible for our own emotions, we become more comfortable with the idea that others are responsible for their own emotions too.

> **It's not your job to manage the emotions of others.**

With this mind-set, we can finally relax—and begin to heal.

The Drama Triangle

Codependents tend to find themselves involved in a lot of dramatic and toxic situations. In order to stop this pattern, we need to let go of this idea that "bad things just keep happening to me, I attract toxic people like a magnet, and nothing can be done about it."

These dramatic situations can usually be explained by the Karpman Drama Triangle—a social model of human interaction created by Stephen B. Karpman in 1968. When someone is made to feel worthless or powerless, they tend to take on the "victim" identity, which makes them feel as if they need to be "rescued," which attracts "rescuers" (who have major issues of their own). Victims also attract more dangerous people, who use charm and sympathy to play the "knight in shining armor" role.

Alternatively, codependents may also become "rescuers" themselves. By saving others and obsessing about their problems, they gain false confidence to distract from their own severely damaged self-worth. This attracts "victims," who will never learn how to be independently happy when they have a "rescuer." The rescuer feels safe, knowing the damaged person needs them. The rescuer also attracts dangerous people, who prey on their constant "giving."

This is often called the "drama triangle," because everyone is distracted from their own unresolved baggage and instead acts out a completely misguided fantasy. It is inevitably doomed to fail, with everyone's negative self-beliefs reinforced. Nobody is growing or learning.

No matter how much the rescuer does, it will never be enough to cure the victim's inner issues, which reinforces the rescuer's fear of "not enough." The rescuer ends up resenting the victim, who will then feel persecuted again, reinforcing their fear of being powerless.

And the cycle repeats itself.

Even though we may view our rescuing in a positive or

heroic light, it is actually accomplishing the opposite. It is protecting the rescued individual from facing their own fears, pains, and failures—the very things that tend to launch true healing and progress. When we insulate someone else from the consequences of their own behavior, we are denying them the chance to grow and learn.

The more I see these dynamics play out, the more I'm convinced both "sides" (victim and rescuer) are meant to meet one another, so they can dance this dance until their protective selves are finally broken. And if not, they dance some more.

Because in the end, nobody wins, everybody loses. The problem is that these are *internal issues* (usually issues that are unknown or unfelt), and the participants are all looking for *external solutions*. We leave this triangle by doing the hard independent work to heal ourselves and release old shame messages.

This is accomplished by slowing down, learning mindfulness, and building a relationship with ourselves. What's going on inside our minds and bodies? What are we so reluctant to feel? What are we hoping someone else will cure instead of doing this work ourselves?

You're the only one who can save yourself.

When we resolve these old painful beliefs, there is no longer anything to "save" or "be saved from." We are unconditionally loved and accepted as we are. Participants in the drama triangle are resistant to that idea. Mindfulness and therapy can help us understand why.

Abusive people use shame and blame to imprint messages

inside you that you are inherently bad and separate from love. Our bodies can do some pretty incredible things to protect us from feeling that pain. But the only way out of this cycle is by feeling the pain, and releasing it.

Those old messages are not true, but they are very real and persistent. No amount of saving or being saved will get rid of them. You're the only one who can save yourself.

Guilt for Having Emotions

There is a great quote from Melody Beatty's classic book *Codependent No More*:

> *"We need to stop telling ourselves we're different for doing and feeling what everyone else does."*

Plenty of people have angry outbursts, irritable moods, weird quirks, and insecurities. If you're a codependent, you likely have no problem with these qualities in other people. You may even find them endearing or sympathetic. Your friends or family could snap at you or be rude, and you'd be unlikely to bat an eye (until you're really at your limit).

But if you have the slightest angry *thought*—not even an action—yourself, you immediately feel guilty about it. Even when you finally gather the courage to talk about a toxic relationship with a friend or therapist, you'll usually feel guilty afterward and wish you hadn't. You're afraid that you've "ruined" everything by finally vocalizing things that your inner voice has been noticing for a long time. Read that again: *You're afraid that you're ruining relationships by acknowledging reality.* As if it's your responsibility to hide or enable another person's unacceptable behavior in order to keep your relationship afloat.

Because the truth is, a lot of your relationships and friendships wouldn't exist anymore if you weren't absorbing problems and pretending everything was fine. Your relationships work because you brush things under the rug, over and over again, until one day it's finally too much and you snap. Then your loved ones wonder what the heck is going on, because from their perspective, everything worked fine and their needs were being met. So why are you suddenly acting so *crazy*!

For this same reason, codependents stay in toxic relationships for far longer than any other person would. Your intuition is actually really good—the problem is, you doubt it. You're so preoccupied with trying to make sure you're reasonable and seeing all perspectives that you fail to throw in the towel when people are blatantly mistreating you. Oftentimes you notice something seems "off" for the longest time, but you feel guilty and dismiss it because the person is nice to you, or because they aren't rejecting you.

Your other friends might meet this same person (for just a few hours) and say: "Wow, they seem weird, I don't want to hang out with them anymore." It is easy for them, because they are not shaming and guilting themselves for noticing negative qualities in another person. They don't feel bad for saying or thinking that. They don't feel obligated to keep seeing that person just because the person acts nice or loving.

You probably noticed the same things as your friends. But you felt guilty about it, or you were afraid to be alone, so you stuck around for months or years of misery.

Codependents worry over and over again that they might be the bad ones, that they might be the ones at fault, that they just need to be a *little* bit more flexible to make things work. But it is this exact worry that lands them in the same situations time and time again. The issue isn't that you "missed" something—the issue is that you continually second-guess yourself, which causes you to stay in situations that others wouldn't tolerate.

Use your mindfulness to explore this sense of guilt and over-responsibility you feel. Over time, you can experiment with letting it go. It is causing you far more trouble than it's worth. You deserve to be in relationships and friendships where your needs are met too. When you stop taking care of others all the time, you give them a chance to meet you halfway. The truly toxic ones won't like this new dynamic and they'll try to manipulate you back to "normal." Again, this is simply a sign that the person isn't a good fit for you anymore.

Conversation with Tony

Tony tends to date and befriend people who need him. He believes that his love can eventually cure any problem his partner is experiencing. He likes to feel appreciated for saving others and he spends all of his time thinking about other people and their problems. He is eternally nice to others, people pleasing and tipping far more than necessary just to see a happy reaction. He loves those small moments of approval. He jumps on any opportunity to offer advice or help. He feels good about himself when he's playing therapist for others. He takes responsibility for their emotions and fantasizes about rescuing them. It's easier to focus on other people's problems because his own emotions feel all "blocked up."

"What does 'blocked up' mean?" I asked. "Where do you feel it in your body?"

"Around here." He motioned over his stomach and chest.

"Your core?"

"Yeah," he said. "I've always felt that way. It's just all twisted up and confused."

"Does anything improve the feeling? Maybe diet or exercise?"

"I feel a lot better when I help people," said Tony. "Like my friends or girlfriend."

"That's really nice! How do you help them?"

"Well, people are always coming to me for help. I'm sort of the rock in my friend group because everyone knows I'll listen and give compassionate advice."

"So people have come to rely on that?"

"Oh, absolutely." He laughed. "Sometimes I'm not sure if they'd be able to function without me. My girlfriend was abused in her childhood, so she really leans on me to feel okay about herself. But it works out perfectly because I love and support her no matter what, when all the other men in her life have abandoned her."

"Does it ever feel overwhelming?" I asked. "Taking care of all those people?"

"No, not at all! I'm happy to help them. They need me. Sometimes I spend all night thinking about ways they can fix their problems. My girlfriend says I'm like the father she never had."

"Where do you think the 'blocked up' feeling fits into all of this?"

"To be honest, I'm not sure," said Tony. "But these people need me because I'm giving them love and support that they've never received before."

"Like emotional support?"

"Not just emotional. My best friend keeps going back to school to pursue new careers, and I've offered to help pay off her debt."

"That's extremely generous of you!"

He beamed. "Thanks, but she deserves it. She's such an amazing person."

"How will you feel if she doesn't complete her courses? Will you be okay with losing that money?"

"Well, she has a history of dropping out, but I think she's going to finish this time. She seems really enthusiastic about it."

"Have you told her that you're planning to help her with this?"

"Not yet," he said. "I want it to be a surprise, because she's had a really tough year and I think this will make her so much happier. I think I'm going to take her out for a nice dinner and tell her then."

"Do you spend a lot of time planning out these ideas?" I asked.

"Oh yeah! If I'm not helping someone, I'm thinking about how I'll help. Everyone says I should be a therapist, because I'm always thinking about other people."

"Do you get a chance to think about yourself sometimes?"

"Sure, but I'm so much better off than most of the people in my life, so I don't mind helping them. I'm stable and successful in my career."

"But what about that 'blocked up' feeling?" I asked. "Have you been able to figure that out?"

He looked frustrated for a moment. "No, but it's not a big deal. It's just a stupid feeling, not the end of the world."

Tony's homework: Stop playing therapist with others. Imagine what you would feel without the approval and appreciation of others. Notice your fantasies about saving people and direct your thoughts inward. Sit instead with the feeling of "blocked up."

C-PTSD

As the name implies, complex PTSD is *complex*. It's still a relatively new area of psychology, and it can be caused or activated by various situations. After emotionally traumatic situations, which sometimes extend for months or even years, sufferers of C-PTSD seem to struggle with a sense of being disconnected from their true selves, blasted into a world dictated by an overactive mind that is constantly analyzing, obsessing, and ruminating. There is often a sense of hypervigilance, being constantly alert and unable to feel vulnerable or safe.

People with C-PTSD also suffer from mood swings, low self-worth, and excessive guilt and worry. They may spend a lot of time thinking about the abuse or trauma that occurred, reliving it every day and repeating their story to others. But no matter how many times they repeat the story, something inside them still feels broken from the experience.

While I've written mostly about abuse-caused C-PTSD in this book, abuse is not a prerequisite for C-PTSD. C-PTSD can also be caused by traumatic situations beyond our control, unfelt grief, and overwhelming guilt—for example, if your loved ones perish in a fire that you accidentally caused, or your child passes away on a vacation that you paid for. These situations may not cause the nightmares and flashbacks seen in traditional PTSD, but they leave you repeating the scenario over and over again, because you are stuck with unbearable guilt and shame. Instead of fully experiencing those things, C-PTSD turns the focus to the external and keeps you hyperfocused on distractions.

C-PTSD sufferers who experienced abuse may engage in mental arguments with their abusers long after the abuse has ended. Most people with C-PTSD experienced ongoing abuse from someone (or multiple people) who repeatedly betrayed their trust, and blamed them for this betrayal. They were made the scapegoat of someone else's shame, which eventually caused them to absorb this shame themselves.

Fantasies of revenge and justice are common. C-PTSD may have you constantly daydreaming about different outcomes of the trauma, how things could have gone better so you would not have ended up in this powerless situation. There is an (understandable) tendency to feel victimized, helpless, and defeated. To explain these difficult sensations, C-PTSD keeps you heavily focused on the *cause* of those feelings—blame, resentment, and the story of abuse.

After dealing with constant invalidation, judgment, and criticism, people with C-PTSD may have learned to stop trusting their own feelings. They may worry that standing up for themselves makes them seem "crazy," or expressing emotions will only lead to ridicule and denial. So instead, they learn to "think" their way into feelings. Everything is a result of careful analysis and reasoning. There is a strong draw toward psychological jargon, diagnoses, and labeling.

Some people with C-PTSD may feel a total lack of energy, exhausted and drained from their experiences. They tend to suffer from depression, anxiety, and sleep disturbances. Others may be blasted in the completely opposite direction—a false burst of manic-like energy that makes them creative, prolific, and expressive. These types tend to be more antagonistic and may feel that they are part of some grand battle of good versus evil. To find meaning from their trauma, they may create communities for people who went through similar trauma, taking on "spreading awareness" as a life mission.

People with C-PTSD may also fantasize about being saved or rescued by a knight in shining armor, a fantasized perfect and loving partner who would help them feel whole again. Alternatively, they might adopt the role of savior themselves, seeking out other wounded people to help. They think if they save enough people, then they might be saved themselves.

But no matter what they do, a wound still remains inside the C-PTSD sufferer that cannot easily be explained or remedied. They often describe feeling as if there are two versions of themselves: before trauma and after trauma. One is carefree, loving, and trusting. The other is fearful, pessimistic, and jaded. They don't know how to reconcile or rejoin these two parts of themselves. They feel more like observers of the world, rather than active participants. They fear that a part of themselves has been broken and can never be put back together.

The Protective Self

Core Wound: Many C-PTSD sufferers dealt with ongoing abuse, minimization, or invalidation. They were blamed for everything, idealized then devalued, and shamed for their emotions. As the name of the disorder implies, their wound is *complex*. Their experiences have caused them to feel powerless and guilty, ashamed of their every thought or emotion. They may deep down believe that everything is their fault.

Protective Self: The protective self that covers this wound is trying to prove the opposite. It is trying to prove that you *do* have power, that you are *not* at fault. It focuses heavily on those that have wronged you, analyzing and understanding everything about them, and proving why their behavior was unacceptable. It fantasizes about justice and making things right. It feels resentment about the unfair things that have happened and ruminates about those experiences frequently.

Dysfunctional Healing Approach: C-PTSD causes the sufferer's thinking to become very rigid and analytical. This was (at some point) a necessary survival skill in order to identify threats and stay safe. However, once the threat is over, those with C-PTSD may still have a lot of trouble "feeling" emotions, and may end up trying to "think" them instead. As they begin recovery, they are likely to use this same analytical and rigid thinking against themselves, embarrassed or impatient by their inability to get in touch with their own feelings. They are also likely to have an extremely negative reaction to the idea of forgiveness, equating that with "letting them win," and seeing forgiveness as something that abusers use to keep hurting victims. And they're not wrong! I'll explore this topic in Part 4 when we come back to forgiveness.

Undoing Blame-Shifting

People with C-PTSD have often been scapegoated by others, either in relationships or throughout their entire childhood. Blame-shifting is when a person does something wrong or inappropriate and then dumps the blame on someone else to avoid taking responsibility for their own behavior. This causes ongoing issues with self-esteem and self-doubt in the person who's been unjustly blamed.

So how can you identify blame-shifting techniques?

1. Playing Victim

This is one of the most common ones. You might ask them to stop criticizing or ridiculing you. Since that situation paints you as a victim, they are quick to turn the tables (because they always need to be the biggest victim). So instead of addressing your legitimate concerns, they bring up (or make up) something completely unrelated from the past where they claim you hurt them. Before you know it, you're the one apologizing to them.

2. Minimizing Your Feelings

If they hurt your feelings, you might calmly express that to them and ask them to stop. They will then laugh at, dismiss, or ridicule your feelings. "You're too sensitive. You're crazy. You're hysterical. You have no sense of humor. Calm down!" The blame is no longer on them for misbehaving, but instead on you for reacting to their misbehavior.

3. Arguing About the Argument

Every argument becomes a metadiscussion about the argument itself, rather than the point you're actually trying to make. They pull you into pointless fights, mincing words and debating semantics in order to put you on the defense. Instead of discussing your legitimate concerns, they comment on your tone and accuse you of doing things they're doing (playing the victim, gaslighting, projecting). The blame is no longer on them, but instead on the way you approached the argument.

4. Guilt Tripping and Pity Stories

If you're prone to feeling sympathy for others, chances are they'll go for this one a lot. If you point out something hurtful they've done, they will start talking about their abusive childhood or an evil ex. Before you know it, you're comforting them, even though they hurt your feelings in the first place. After all, how can you be mad at someone when they open up to you about something so traumatic? *(Hint: That's the whole point.)* Everyone goes through trials and tribulations. But healthy individuals don't use those experiences as excuses to harm others, and they certainly don't bring up those pity stories to conveniently avoid taking responsibility for their behavior.

5. The Stink Bomb

This is the last resort, usually when they've been blatantly caught or called out for something they know they did wrong. And so they throw a completely unfounded, terrible accusation at you. You thought you had a slam-dunk case. Proof. Evidence. Everything. And then they come back with this:

- Well, you abused me.
- You hit me.
- You assaulted me.
- You cheated on me.
- You never loved me.
- You're mentally ill.
- You're stalking me.

Suddenly your slam-dunk case isn't such a slam dunk anymore. Now you're defending yourself against wild accusations that you never could have even dreamed of. Who could prepare for that?

And once again, that's the whole point. The blame is now off them, and suddenly you're the one in hot water.

What can you do?

When someone blame-shifts like this, there is an (understandable) temptation to explain yourself, defend your name, and prove your point. But the problem is, this is exactly what they want you to do. They blame-shift so you'll react. They often accuse you of doing things that they themselves are doing, and because it's so infuriating, you just have to say something. But again, that's the point.

By sucking you into these arguments, they are consuming your energy and watching you progressively self-destruct, so they can use your reactions to prove their own point ("Wow, look how bitter and angry you are!").

Al-Anon is a program for partners of addicts and alcoholics, but many of their resources apply to manipulative relationships as well. If you go to an Al-Anon meeting, you'll probably hear someone say "Don't JADE!" The term "JADE" stands for "justify, argue, defend, explain." When you try to defend yourself against a false accusation, you legitimize it by even acknowledging it. The only way to respond to these tactics is to stand up and walk away.

Odds are, you are an unusually reasonable person who is always trying to see things from everyone else's perspective. You constantly worry that you're being unfair ("Oh no, what if I actually am this terrible thing they're accusing me of?"), which makes you a prime target for people like this. Because unfortunately, in all your worry and self-doubt about being unfair, you fail to see situations that are *actually unfair*—to you.

Blame-shifting leaves long-lasting feelings of resentment and powerlessness in the target. You begin to feel that there is no justice in the world—that abusive people can just get away with anything, and you have to absorb it all because there is no other way out. It feels unfair and wrong, like you're never allowed to express an opinion or point out the truth. Because when you do so, you're met with such vitriol and contempt that it becomes unsafe. So you are trapped, and justice is not served.

How to Win Against an Abuser?

I get this question all the time, and my answer is always the same: Don't try to win. As soon as we engage in this win/lose mentality, we abandon our hearts and forget what's really important: vulnerability and love.

Yes, absolutely you should remove toxic people from your life, but it should be from the perspective of self-love, not "winning." As long as we maintain this false illusion of control, we're still connected to the person in our psyches. A hallmark of C-PTSD is fantasizing about gaining some power over an otherwise powerless situation.

Recovery should not be about proving you don't care. Presumably if you were this deeply hurt, it's because you cared a lot. Just because abusers dismiss, shame, and ridicule that care does not mean you need to pretend you don't care. Just because they gain a temporary burst of energy from watching you suffer does not mean you should see your own suffering as "victory" to them. Who cares if it's a victory to them? It's still real. The only thing that matters is restoring your own ability to love, attach, and be vulnerable. This simply cannot happen when we're trying to "win."

It's strange, because abusive people will insult you for "taking so long to get over it" while they've gone decades without "getting over" their own abusive habits. I don't say that to be rude;

I'd happily root for any abuser who seeks therapy. But the fact is, most don't. Instead they just sit there judging other people for being "victims," while they themselves are sitting on a mountain of their own unresolved psychological damage.

So turn your focus from external to internal and ask yourself what you're actually feeling inside. When someone cheats on you, blames you, betrays you, replaces you, dumps you . . . the normal emotions are inadequacy, worthlessness, and rejection. It's okay and good to feel those things. Nurturing these feelings back to health is how we find our way home.

Turn your focus from external to internal.

There is absolutely nothing wrong with thinking: "I loved this person with all my heart, and I am hurting right now." If they see that as a victory, who cares? At least you are being honest with yourself. You do not need anger or resentment to maintain No Contact with someone. Self-love and vulnerability are far more effective motivators, because when you recover that soft place in your heart, you would never want to put it in harm's way.

When we sit there counting No Contact days as a badge of honor, fantasizing about how much it must upset them, it's a complete waste of our focus and energy. Winning and justice may be what your protective self wants, but love and authenticity is what your heart longs for.

If you went the ego route, be kind to yourself. This is the default, expected human reaction to intense rejection and jealousy. Also, half the time you're not even able to experience your real feelings because they got numbed out by C-PTSD. Are you really going to judge yourself for that? I prefer to see it as an act of love and protection by the body. Switching over to heart mode can only happen when you are unconditionally kind and forgiving to yourself. Start the moment you're ready, perhaps right now.

C-PTSD or Borderline?

There is some overlap between these two conditions, which often causes C-PTSD sufferers to wonder if they might have BPD as well. Especially after cluster-B abuse, it's common for individuals to display some symptoms of cluster-B disorders themselves. Please do not diagnose yourself with a personality disorder because of your behavior in the aftermath of a traumatic situation. This is something only a trained professional should do, and you should also give yourself some time to heal from the situation before determining if your symptoms are an anomaly or part of a larger pattern.

If you *do* have BPD, there's a whole section of the book for that. And you might resonate with a lot of these C-PTSD symptoms as well. The National Institutes of Health (NIH) recently published an interesting study comparing the symptoms of BPD and C-PTSD. Here are the overlapping symptoms:

- Mood shifts
- Guilt
- Low self-worth
- Feeling disconnected

But here are some BPD symptoms that we don't usually see in C-PTSD:

- Episodes of rage
- Self-harm
- Impulsiveness
- Unstable sense of self (lack of identity)
- Unstable relationships (extreme idealization and devaluation)
- Frantic attempts to avoid real or imagined abandonment

People with C-PTSD tend to despise drama and conflict, to the point of being avoidant. They seek out consistency and stability. Boring is A-OK with them. They avoid problematic exes and are happy with one romantic focus. They may be hypervigilant and anxious, attempting to maintain as much harmony in their life as possible, even if it means being alone. They are often shy and polite to others, getting along fine with coworkers and friends. They may be extremely hesitant about sharing their emotions with others, keeping everything so guarded that they seem calm even when their inner world is falling apart.

People with BPD may say "I hate drama," but it seems to appear in their life quite frequently, because peace and calm are uncomfortable to them. They tend to sabotage any consistency or stability that enters their life. They keep their exes around as much as possible, even people they declared abusive or evil. They have significant issues with coworkers and friends, repeatedly getting into intense crisis situations and therapist-like dynamics that later cause them trouble. They have a lot of difficulty containing or controlling their emotions, bursting into tears or rage around people they barely know.

Conversation with Anna

Anna feels separate and isolated from everyone around her. She blogs frequently about the man who abused her, socializing only with others who have been abused by similar men. She has constant fantasies in which the man who harmed her is finally brought to justice. She also reimagines the past and sees herself standing up to him, rather than being abused by him. She takes on multiple causes to help others and bring more justice to the world, especially ones that focus on good versus evil. She dreams about a perfect partner who will appear and save her. All of these things distract her from a feeling in her heart that she can't describe.

"Can you tell me more about the feeling in your heart?" I asked Anna.

"What does that have to do with anything?" She raised her eyebrows. "Listen, I have a few things I wanted to talk about today. My blog has gotten really popular and I wanted to run an idea by you."

"Sure."

"I've decided I want to turn some of my articles into a book!" she said. "I'll probably self-publish, and I'm hoping to get it out there next year."

"That's so cool!" I said. "What's the book about?"

"A guidebook for empaths on how to survive and avoid evil," she said. "There are just so many dangerous people out there, and I want to help empaths learn how to spot them."

"Wow, that sounds like quite a project!"

"Yes, and I think the time is right, because we seem to have reached a breaking point between good and evil."

"What do you mean?"

"As a world, it seems like everything is coming to fruition—like a battle."

"I wrote a chapter in *Psychopath Free* like that!" I laughed at the coincidence. "It's wild how this stuff blasts us into these big-picture battles."

"What do you mean *this stuff*?" she asked.

"Well, you said you have a weird feeling in your heart, and you also see the world as a big battle. That's the same exact combination I experienced."

Again she raised her eyebrows. "What do the two have to do with each other?"

"In my experience, the big-picture perspective was keeping me focused on grandiose battles and fantasies, because it kept me away from the feeling in my heart."

"But the feeling in my heart isn't bad. It's just . . . weird."

"Exactly! That's the whole point of the big fantasies. They keep your mind focused externally, so the true pain in the body stays numbed out. So you can feel *weird* instead of *bad*."

"So you're saying the feeling in my heart is actually painful?" she asked skeptically. "Even though I don't feel any pain right now?"

"That's right," I said. "The heart is where we're supposed to feel love, right?"

"Wait a minute." She laughed. "You feel love in the organ that pumps blood?"

"Well, let's try it another way. Where do you feel excitement?"

"In my stomach, I guess. You know, butterflies."

"Okay, and where do you feel anxiety?"

She thought for a moment. "My core tightens up, and my hands start to sweat."

"So those are all feelings associated with parts of your body, right?"

"I guess."

"Okay, and love is associated with the heart—it always has been—because that's where love is physically felt in the body. Is love what you feel in your heart right now?"

Suddenly her expression sank, and she looked down.

"No." She paused. "It just feels hollow and numb."

Anna's homework: Take a step back from the justice causes and awareness missions. If you fantasize about a perfect partner coming to save you, imagine what you would have to feel if that person never appeared. Sit instead with the hollow feeling.

Avoidant

People with avoidant personality disorder (AVPD) can be some of the most pleasant people in the world, if you're their friend or colleague or family member. But for the avoidants, it's not so pleasant. They tend to be very agreeable and polite, despising any sort of drama or conflict. Unfortunately, their aversion to conflict is often at the sacrifice of boundaries, resulting in them being surrounded by exactly the type of people who make them uncomfortable. As a result, it becomes easier to just seclude themselves and exist largely in isolation.

People with AVPD are afraid of taking up too much space, so they end up taking up far too little space, making themselves smaller and smaller until they just feel like friendly robots. But no matter how "nice" they are, they're still always worried and anxious about what others might think of them, terrified of humiliation and ridicule. So instead, they constantly validate and listen to others, which attracts people who take up *way* too much space.

It is not uncommon for avoidants to end up in friendships or relationships with people who suffer from BPD, and end up listening to dramatic stories for hours on end while barely getting a word in themselves. When they do speak, they worry that they've spoken too much and usually wish they hadn't said anything at all. At least if they're quiet, they won't do anything embarrassing. They doubt themselves constantly and fail to see how uneven the communication is in their interpersonal relationships.

People with AVPD can be very imaginative, often sharing

their most authentic feelings through creative expression. By existing in their fantasy worlds, they don't need to take part in their own frustrating reality. They may dream of a perfect happy future, imagining situations where they are finally at peace. They may project parts of themselves into fictional characters, because it is easier to imagine other people expressing intense emotions than to actually experience them.

They tend to be unaware of their deepest feelings, especially anything perceived as a "negative" emotion. Things like jealousy or anger are terrifying, because they might make you seem "crazy," which would only lead to humiliation. But jealousy and anger serve important purposes: to help you understand when your needs are not being met, and teach you the lessons needed to get those needs met. When we repress these feelings, we repress our needs. We end up surrounded by people who believe their needs to be more important than our own.

My goal is to help you understand the underlying fears that drive avoidant behavior, so that you can let them go and feel comfortable taking up some more space. Additionally, by learning to welcome your emotions (rather than worry that they make you crazy), you can finally start getting your needs met and find more balanced relationships.

The Protective Self

Core Wound: Like most protective selves, the avoidant wound seems to be largely based around a wound of rejection—specifically, any kind of humiliation or ridicule. These are shame-based experiences that can leave long-lasting imprints. While you may long for meaningful human contact deep down, the protective self is too afraid to experience genuine emotions. It worries that expressing emotions (especially negative ones) will cause you to seem crazy and be judged by others, pushing them away.

Protective Self: The AVPD protective self is extremely polite, quiet, and agreeable. By being nice to everyone, it aims to ensure that the wound is never reactivated. No one can humiliate the protective self if it is constantly presenting a friendly face to the world. Similar to codependents, it is quick to sacrifice its own wants and needs in order to appease others. But unlike codependents, it does not express any sort of neediness. If it senses even a hint of rejection, it simply withdraws. Eventually it withdraws so much that there is very little human contact, and instead spends time engaged in fantasies and imagination.

Dysfunctional Healing Approach: The avoidant protective self will attempt to approach healing in a way that does not involve expressing any uncomfortable or negative emotions. It will quickly try to forgive everyone else, hoping this will remove all of the "icky" anger. Much of the healing may be attempted through creative outlets and imagining fictional scenarios, rather than through the avoidant individuals themselves.

Conversation with a Therapist

Below I share my own experiences with avoidant qualities that came up in therapy. A few years ago, I had built up an elaborate fantasy world of characters and settings. I imagined these characters interacting with each other, and I had surges of excitement and inspiration when I came up with a new plot twist. I related to my own thoughts and feelings as characters, since I seemed unable to feel them myself. In reality, all I could really feel was that vague tightness in my chest described earlier.

"When did you first experience this tightness?" my therapist asked.

"I don't know," I said. "It was some time after my first relationship ended. But that was five years ago and I never think about it anymore."

"What happened in the relationship?"

"I was completely in love with him," I said. "But he cheated on me with some other guy. It was going on for months and I never even knew about it. He eventually dumped me for the other guy and reached out later to tell me how happy he was."

"That's terrible," she said. "It must have taken a long time to heal from a first relationship like that. You must have felt very angry."

"Not really," I said. "I was acting like a lunatic, but my best friend at the time told me it was my fault. If I got angry, she shook her head and said my ex was awesome. She said I needed to analyze what I did to cause the experience. She set up private meetings with our mutual friends to discuss my issues. If I cried, she looked at me with disgust and ignored me, so I tried to just get over things quickly."

My therapist raised her eyebrows. "So her opinion was . . . important to you?"

"She was studying to be a psychology major," I said. "She just seemed like she knew something bad about me that I didn't know. And I really was acting like a total nutjob, I'm not exaggerating."

"And sometime in there, the tightness in your chest started."

"Yeah."

"Is it constant?"

"Yes," I said. "It's always there."

"Does it hurt?"

"No," I said. "It's just tight. It doesn't feel bad or anything. I'm completely fine otherwise. I spend a lot of time alone, but I'm happy. I write stories, I have nice friends, and I like my job. I love listening to music when I fantasize about my stories and characters."

"Can you tell me about your stories?"

"Well, the one I'm working on lately is a political thriller about a congressman running for president. He had a big sexting scandal in the past, sort of like Anthony Weiner. But the story isn't really about him, it's about the people he hurt."

"That sounds interesting," she said. "Who are the characters?"

"It has three perspectives. One is the congressman's ex-wife, Annie. She left him after the scandal and lives alone in the mountains. She's got a lot of love to give, really funny and kind. But she also has some lingering anger issues that make her act crazy sometimes. She's sort of on a big revenge kick."

"How about the other two?"

"Phil is the husband of the mistress from the sexting scandal. He's seriously emasculated from the whole thing, deals with a lot of inadequacy and inferiority."

"That makes sense after what he went through," she said. "And who's the last character?"

"The therapist, Stacey. She means well, but she's everybody's least favorite character. She's constantly diagnosing people with mental disorders. She just judges and criticizes everyone. Total control freak, you know?"

"She sounds unpleasant," she said. "All right, so I know this will probably spoil things, but I'm curious what happens with the characters?"

"Well, Annie ends up meeting Phil, and they fall in love."

"That's nice!"

"Yeah, it takes a while. Annie basically sees that Phil is hurting too, which softens her anger a lot. She decides to put aside her vendetta about the scandal, so she can take care of him."

"And what about Stacey?"

"They leave her behind, but there aren't any hard feelings."

"Your characters seem to have a lot of complex emotions," she said. "Were they inspired by your own anger and inadequacy?"

"No," I said, confused. "Like I told you, I'm happy. I don't have those kind of emotions."

Jackson's homework: Take a step back from the fantasy worlds, characters, and plots. When your mind convinces you to dive back into an exciting world or character idea, don't get caught up. Focus instead on the tight feeling. Explore how the fantasies are manifesting themselves in writing and artwork. Search for any messages that the body may be trying to communicate to you.

Borderline

Borderline personality disorder (BPD) is one of the more challenging and interesting protective selves. From the National Institute of Mental Health: "Borderline personality disorder (BPD) is a serious mental disorder marked by a pattern of ongoing instability in moods, behavior, self-image, and functioning. These experiences often result in impulsive actions and unstable relationships. A person with BPD may experience intense episodes of anger, depression, and anxiety that may last from only a few hours to days."

Like most personality disorders, BPD is still in the early phases of being researched and understood. There are various debates around whether the disorder can be "cured," with most treatments offering different combinations of symptom management and medication. These often involve very regimented and structured approaches—teaching you how to manage or talk yourself out of certain emotions that come up, which makes it hard to trust your own emotions. Like noticing when deep anger or jealousy symptoms arise, and choosing not to act on them. But I don't want you to spend your life learning how to repress or self-validate deeply uncomfortable sensations. My goal with this book is not to manage symptoms, but rather to resolve the underlying wound that *causes* the symptoms.

In order to do this, we need to become aware of the protective self as soon as possible.

I understand that people suffering from BPD are greatly comforted by validation and sympathy, but these things only seem to strengthen the protective self's hold over the sufferer. It's like an alcoholic seeking alcohol, but validation and sympathy sound much more sweet. The problem is, the validation and sympathy are never enough. The BPD protective self will *never* be satisfied, it will always be doubting and testing, seeking more external validation.

And so this book will take a different approach to the disorder. While I do empathize with the deep suffering felt by people with BPD, I am going to be as direct as possible in my writing. Because as long as the BPD protective self is running the show, they will be running in circles forever. It is not uncommon for people with BPD to suddenly think they are "healed" or have a dozen breakthroughs in therapy, only to be followed a week later by feelings of worthlessness and self-loathing. So the goal here is not to suddenly feel cured, but instead to slow down and become aware of *how* we approach healing. With BPD, there is often an immediate and manic excitement about new healing ideas, soon followed by boredom and giving up.

In the coming chapters, I will not be coddling the BPD protective self because it is *not who you truly are.* Instead, I want you to non-judgmentally become aware of how it operates, and why it operates that way. The more you do this, the less attached you become to that part of yourself—the less you "identify" with it. And that is exactly the goal, because it is *not* your identity. It is a work-around your body put in place to protect you.

In addition to this book, I highly recommend dialectical behavioral therapy (DBT), which will teach you invaluable tools for managing difficult feelings. If at any point you're experiencing thoughts of suicide, please put this book down and call emergency services.

I also want to say that people with BPD are *fantastic* candidates for spirituality. You have strong imaginations and a constant desire for unconditional love, which never seems to be fulfilled by relationships. That's exactly what "God" is—infinite unconditional love. As long as you don't use spirituality to feed the protective self, spirituality can become a wonderful and fulfilling part of your life. Replacing overcharged emotional energy with spiritual energy brings a natural lightness that calms everything down.

As you focus more on your own relationship with unconditional love, you will become less obsessed and hyperfocused on your relationships with others. Rather than requiring other people for your own worth (and therefore constantly being aware or paranoid of their every move), you will find that your worth comes from within. This shift from external to internal naturally leads you to behave in new ways that make people *want* to stick around, without you needing to be perfect or mirror them.

You will make yourself miserable trying to explain everything with analytical psychological terms. Human beings aren't meant to be under a microscope like that. Spirituality makes a really nice companion to therapy, because it provides love and warmth that you can tap into any time.

As you explore this unconditional love, you are likely to come to the source of the problem: something in you *resists* the love. So often, people with BPD don't believe they can be loved, so they're constantly searching for external validation of their worth. With a broken inner gauge, there is a heavy reliance on the outside world and other people. This leads to "testing" others, to see just how much they're willing to put up with and prove how much they care for you. Codependents are the only people who tend to stick around past the first few tests, but no amount of love or sympathy is ever enough to fill the void of the BPD protective self. Inevitably everyone will "fail" the test, and the protective self can safely reaffirm its own beliefs that everyone abandons you, or that people have "always hated" you.

With BPD, there seems to be no middle ground—you are either all perfect (the idealizer) or the shameful mess (the devaluer). You think if you behave 100 percent correctly, becoming exactly what everyone else wants, then you will be happy. You do everything right, you're the most romantic partner on the planet, or the most desirable employee a boss has ever interviewed. But inevitably the demon inside ends up bubbling over and you expose a different part of yourself. You have an episode, and you feel ashamed or disgusted with yourself, as if you've ruined your entire dynamic with this person because you no longer appear "perfect." You know and assume that they see you differently now—that you've lost your perfect status. With this disgust of yourself comes disgust of others. It is easier to assume others have become boring or bad, rather than face the common denominator of your own patterns. Instead of experiencing your shame, your protective self begins telling you stories about how others have behaved badly or how others are in the wrong.

There is this fantasized belief that if *someone*, just one person, would understand and sympathize with you enough—*then* you would be happy. If they would just love you through all of the drama, sobbing, and emotions—*then* you would finally be happy. This is, of course, never enough. Even if you find the perfect partner who loves you no matter what, there is still a wound inside of you that prevents you from accepting or believing their love. So the protective self is constantly fantasizing about being saved or rescued, romanticizing tragic situations and even wishing to be injured so someone could swoop in to save the day.

When first beginning early recovery, you may find it really hard to differentiate between actual stories and exaggerated fantasies of the protective self. It's not necessarily intentional lying or dishonesty, it's just what the protective self does. For example, the BPD protective self can quickly escalate from "my boss asked me to come in early tomorrow" to "my boss is a slave driver who screamed at me that I'm worthless and if I don't come in early tomorrow, I'm fired." Then the protective self desperately tells this story to anyone who will listen, with each retelling becoming more dramatic and tragic, seeking external validation until you actually believe that's what happened. Eventually, this gives you all the fuel you need to quit your job, which may have been the underlying goal all along.

Deep down, people with BPD know that many of their problems are self-caused, but acknowledging this can lead them down a dark hole of fear and shame. So the immediate reaction is to avoid that uncomfortable feeling and construct another crisis or victim situation to explain the problem. Unfortunately, in blocking away shame, we also block healthy self-doubts and logical perceptions of reality, which give us the opportunity to learn and grow from our mistakes.

To offer another example, a compulsive shopper who's in tremendous debt *knows* deep down that they have caused this problem, but their shame is so uncomfortable that they continue to distract from it with more shopping. They are blocked away from the reasonable part of themselves that could simply say, "Hey, this is a problem and I can fix it." Instead, it takes them down an intolerable path of "This is a problem and it's all my fault because I'm a horrible human being with no hope of redemption." That is not a sustainable sensation to sit with, so instead, it all gets numbed away—as does any hope of fixing the problem.

If you read any of this and feel a sort of dread or shame like,

"Oh God, I do that. I'm so evil and bad!," that's the *exact* sensation I'm suggesting you explore. Do not shove aside this feeling or try to distract from it. I know it feels so uncomfortable, but it's actually a good thing. The protective self is hardwired to do *anything* to escape the sensation of shame. Now the protective self has been "noticed," and it really doesn't like that. Fortunately, it's the beginning of your journey to freedom.

The Protective Self

> Core Wound: People with BPD tend to be suffering from a deep wound of rejection or abandonment, which has planted an idea of inner defectiveness in them. This causes them to believe they are inherently worthless and unlovable—that they cannot be themselves, because no one will ever want that person. Note: People with BPD often think "being themselves" equates to being extremely emotional and sobbing, or being clingy and jealous, or manic and impulsive. So the protective self is on its best behavior (idealization period) until it feels safe, and then exposes these more and more dramatic qualities, until eventually people leave. But neither of these sides is who you truly are. They are both the protective self, one "perfect" and another "broken." The protective self creates an infinite loop to keep you trapped and justify its own existence.

Protective Self: The borderline and narcissistic protective selves are some of the most difficult to penetrate. Because the core wound was so painful, their bodies tend to numb out those sensations and make them "inaccessible" in the brain, masking them with boredom and emptiness. The protective self is preoccupied with receiving sympathy, attention, and adoration from others. It is dramatic and overemotional. It lacks a stable identity of its own, so it becomes obsessed with others. The protective self always wants to be the victim, to feel persecuted and wronged. It strongly resonates with the "suffering pain" identity. It wants to be the biggest sufferer, and feels deeply uncomfortable when others receive sympathy for their suffering, thinking "but mine is worse." It frequently takes action to ensure that others see you as the ultimate victim. It has difficulty addressing its own mistakes or inappropriate behaviors, because it immediately jumps to telling pity stories to *explain* the mistakes. It constantly believes that others "hate" you, even people you don't know. The BPD protective self *reinforces itself* by sabotaging important relationships, so that it can prove to you that everyone always abandons you, and therefore you *need* its protection. It's like a burglar selling home safety alarms.

Dysfunctional Healing Approach: The borderline protective self will keep you running on a hamster wheel until you notice how it operates. It will approach healing in an overly dramatic, self-pitying way. It uses therapy to constantly revisit trauma stories, and even invents stories along the way. It is always searching for some sort of tragic story to *explain* the inner discomfort, rather than just *feeling* the inner discomfort. It will have constant "revelations" and keep "processing the past" forever. It will think that everything needs to be about sobbing and healing the inner child. It may offer "forgiveness" to others but still ruminate and resent for years. The protective self might attempt to apologize or forgive others, and then feel angry and victimized if it is not well received. Additionally, it tends to use therapists for external validation and sympathy, rather than focusing on the underlying emptiness.

The Borderline Cycle of Oversharing and Rejection

Relationships and close friendships are extremely challenging when you have borderline personality disorder. Oftentimes this stems from oversharing and emotional unloading. Individuals with BPD can be a lot of fun and charming at first, but once they become comfortable, they begin treating everyone as their therapist and talk constantly about trauma, abuse, or crisis stories. Or they complain about all their exes and friends that previously abandoned them. Or they push boundaries with emotional outbursts or inappropriate flirting. Then people start backing away and confirm their worst fears. The cycle tends to go like this:

- Meet a new person and get super excited about them (to the point of obsession, waiting anxiously for their every text).
- Mirror and flatter them; you seem to get along great.
- Finally, you've found someone you can trust! They won't abandon and betray you like everyone else. So you share your past trauma, childhood issues, and fears with them. Surely that will enhance your bond with them and help them see you as sympathetic.
- They start withdrawing or distancing themselves.
- Everyone says "don't worry about it," so you try not to worry. Maybe you practice some DBT or mindfulness techniques to convince yourself it's not "happening again."
- Your suspicions end up being true; they stop talking to you altogether.
- You think to yourself: "This world is so cruel and hates emotions and vulnerability! I am alone and will always be alone, because everyone I love abandons me."
- You complain to others about this latest abandonment. They say, "You didn't need that jerk anyway! Just find new friends who accept you for who you really are."
- Repeat the cycle.

Borderline individuals are essentially living out their own self-fulfilling prophecy on infinite repeat. They say and do things that "test" the relationship, hoping others will prove their loyalty. But it is never enough, because the protective self is *never* satisfied. With no true sense of self, it constantly relies on the approval and validation of others in order to feel "okay."

The problem here is that healthy individuals put boundaries in place because they do not wish to play the rescuer role. And so as the person with BPD tests, overshares, or reacts emotionally, the healthy individual withdraws. This is interpreted as "abandonment," but that is simply not the case. It is an *adult* making an *adult* decision to leave another *adult*.

Tragically, the borderline protective self continues to sabotage stability and peace so that it can justify its own existence. It may feel like abandonment or betrayal, but you must not live your life waiting for "the one person" who won't abandon you "like everyone else." The protective self is tricking you. It has everything backward. A long time ago, you may have been rejected or abandoned for reasons that had nothing to do with you. But in the present moment, your protective self is largely responsible for the "abandonment" you continue to experience. Here are some reasons why:

1. Viewing others as your savior or rescuer (or long-lost parent figure) pushes away healthy individuals, and attracts partners with codependent or disordered tendencies. It's totally fine to share something you're dealing with, if you're taking steps to deal with it yourself. As in, not desperately needing reassurance or advice from others to cope. But healthy people will not want to become your therapist—that doesn't make them heartless,

and it doesn't mean they're abandoning you. It just means they have healthy boundaries, which can be very uncomfortable to someone with borderline personality.

2. Loudly sobbing or yelling in front of people pushes away healthy individuals and potential new friends. It's good to shed tears over something sad in front of someone. People aren't turned away by that. They're turned away by overdramatic crying, which borders on screaming. When every trivial situation is upgraded to "abuse" or "crisis," this can quickly become exhausting to even the most patient friend. Eventually, rather than sympathize with these never-ending sad stories, they'll want you to learn how to support and validate yourself. If we view ourselves as victims, then we see others as either rescuers or perpetrators (or both). Healthy people don't want to play those roles.

3. Sharing trauma in an attempt to bond in a deep, sympathetic way is not a healthy way to connect with others. People with BPD often meet someone new and quickly (within a few hours, days, or weeks) tell them about their life story, trauma, abusive exes, mentally ill parents. This is a quick turnoff for emotionally healthy people, not because they don't sympathize with your plight, but because it's been unloaded way too quickly. Friends are not meant to be therapists. However, it's totally fine to open up about your issues with trusted

loved ones, if you are not trying to use it for bonding, or testing them to see if they're "sympathetic enough." Ask yourself *why* you are sharing this—it is almost always sympathy seeking, so others see you in a certain way (the protective self wants to be perceived as the victim), so they'll soothe and comfort you. The truth is, if we do the hard work to actually heal our trauma, there is very little desire to share it constantly with others. Sometimes we subconsciously prefer to carry it as a badge of honor, worshipping our suffering as if it defines us. And this is what leads to the classic borderline mentality: *"If I confide intimate personal details to this person, it will make us closer."* But it won't. It puts the other person in an impossible situation. If they're kind and understanding, it will intensify your infatuation. If they implement proper firm boundaries, you will feel abandoned and rejected.

4. Extreme shifts between fun and loving to bitter and raging can be very overwhelming to others. During the idealization period, you may become quickly infatuated and obsessed with a new person, desperately waiting for their next text and trying to figure out how to be their perfect friend. You mirror them, copy their personality, and try to be the best friend or partner possible. But inevitably your other side slips out, and you find yourself having episodes or leaning too heavily on them. When they start backing away, you feel abandoned and betrayed, as though people only love you when you're

"perfect." But no one *asked* you to be perfect, you *chose* to do that up front because you believed it was the only way people would love you. Then eventually you burn out, drop the mask, and act out. Then people leave and the protective self says, "Oh my God, people always leave me when I'm not perfect." But that's not the truth.

If you are actually feeling suicidal, you must go to therapy or call the police. Those are the only two sensible options. Expecting others to take care of us through that is unfair.

Here is why I love mindfulness: it teaches us how to love and calm ourselves, so we don't require other people to do it for us. That is a turnoff to healthy people. Healthy people love themselves, and freely share love with people who love themselves. Of course they offer comfort and sympathy during difficult times, but not as a daily routine.

With mindfulness, you go from the extremes described above, to having much more interest in your inner experience, which causes much less obsession with what others think, which gets rid of all the paranoia and fear that turns people away to begin with.

You're able to share your vulnerable self with people without resorting to dramatic sobbing and "Oh my God, thank you so much for saving me, you're such a beautiful soul!" Instead, we actually *work* on our issues, we save *ourselves*, so sharing is done in a much calmer, relaxed—even humorous—way.

This nightmare cycle repeats itself because of the BPD individual's behavior, not because they are unlucky or victims of the world, or because everyone hates emotions and vulnerability. It's just not true. If you want the cycle to stop, you can start taking the steps to change.

The alternative is to believe you are a powerless victim of this cruel heartless world, which absolutely ensures that the cycle repeats itself and reaffirms your beliefs, which are a self-fulfilling prophecy.

When we start to focus on loving ourselves (rather than getting hyperexcited about other people), we become much more relaxed with new friendships. Because we enjoy them, rather than needing them and trying to act perfect. When we give off the relaxed vibe, people are always happy to be friends. But this has to be authentic, not trying to act cool when we feel frenzied internally.

Love is not receiving external validation and reassurance. It is not becoming a perfect match for someone else. It is not other people sympathizing with trauma. It is not manically seeing others as the magical solution to everything. Love is different, and we're going to find it.

The Favorite Person

In the online BPD world, there is a concept called the "favorite person" (FP). It's basically a person that the BPD individual becomes obsessed with, mirroring, flattering, caretaking, and idealizing. It is not necessarily their romantic partner—it can also be a close friend or peer. Those with BPD use their FP as a source for their own identity. They spend most of their time thinking about this person, offer gifts and favors, and become devastated if the person takes too long to reply to a text message. They become jealous if their FP makes new friends or takes on a separate hobby. The favorite person is the *biggest distraction* from BPD recovery. It's like heroin to a heroin addict. Those with BPD fantasize about this perfect ideal person, hoping for unconditional love and acceptance, because they do not love and accept *themselves* as they are.

The core issue with BPD is a wounded inner world, so the inner world is shut down (emptiness, numbness), resulting in hyperobsession with the *external* world. Having an FP fuels this disordered thinking and distracts BPD sufferers from experiencing their inner world.

Can heroin addicts recover when they're actively using heroin? Of course not. For BPD, external obsessions *are* the drug, and they need to be diminished in order to begin true recovery. How in the world can you find your true self when you are frantically modifying yourself to become someone else's "perfect" non-abandonable mirror image?

Mindfulness and DBT can help you notice every time you get manically excited or obsessed about another person, idea, career path, dream, sexual encounter, spending spree, crisis story, identity change . . . And it can help you *decline* those compulsions and instead *stay* with the intolerable feelings that surface when you don't take action. Emptiness and boredom are psychological defenses. They numb you and convince you to "do" something, which keeps you distracted from the pain. Mindfulness helps you notice this trickery.

Getting in touch with these feelings, what lives behind the emptiness, and learning how to *love* it all, is how we heal the inner world. It's incredibly scary at first because it feels so painful and real, like it could kill us. And it *is* real, but we can't heal it until we stay with it—stay with our bodies, rather than allowing our minds to continue doing psychological gymnastics to distract and protect us from experiencing our wound. The more time we spend feeling the wound, the more we develop the skills and awareness needed to realize those scary feelings *aren't even true.*

You are not evil, or bad, or a fraud, or hopeless, or irreparably damaged, or inadequate, or worthless, or fake, or separate from love. Seriously, you're not. You might have made bad decisions or behaved badly or had bad thoughts *because* of those feelings living inside of you. But *you* are not bad. I can tell you this a million times (external), your FP can tell you this a million times (external), and maybe you'll feel good for a bit (distraction). But it'll never last, because the belief still lives inside of you (internal), and you are the *only* one who can do the extremely difficult work to release this from your body.

When you read my words above, maybe you got super excited, but then a dreadful sinking feeling took over that said: *"No, he's wrong. I'm not good. I'm the exception. I'm secretly terrible and I just need to admit it. I have done terrible things that are beyond forgiveness." That's* the "monster" in you that needs your help. If a child said those things to you about themselves, would you shove them away and hide from them, or would you offer them comfort and compassion to help them realize it's not true? You'd help them, right?

It can take many months or years of mindfulness practice to accept this and rewire our brains. Once we restore a healthy relationship with ourselves, however, the external obsessions melt away. We no longer seek or desire constant sympathy, validation, infatuation, reassurance, and attention. Those things actually become very uncomfortable because they impede the healthy relationship we've built with ourselves.

Instead, we are finally introduced to the type of love, bonding, and attachment that we always longed for.

Rather than searching for a new FP, this might be a great time to explore therapy and DBT, so that you can find your true identity. Probably someone in your life took up way too much "space," made you an extension of themselves, and shamed your true identity. It could take months or years of extended trauma work and mindfulness, but it is a journey worth taking.

Romanticizing Mental Illness

There is a growing movement of people who wish to exempt personality disordered individuals from any criticism, claiming that it stigmatizes mental illness. But we need to be clear about where the stigma comes from. People with *untreated* personality disorders are often criticized because they tend to cause a hugely disproportionate amount of damage in their interpersonal relationships.

There's a reason you don't see communities devoted to healing from relationships with people who have ADHD or diabetes. Because the need isn't there, because those people don't cause a disproportionate amount of damage to their partners.

No amount of cheerleader love or social justice protection will improve the disorder. In fact, it only serves as a distraction, and continues feeding the protective self with stories of persecution and victimhood, rather than getting started on the path of personal responsibility.

Stigmatization is not the cause of personality disorders. If external love and acceptance cured personality disorders, they wouldn't exist anymore. These are people who are deeply suffering (often without knowing it), and they need to find their true selves in order to begin to truly heal.

People with BPD do not need cheerleaders or another "favorite person." They need professionals who truly get it, nonjudgmentally hold them accountable for their inappropriate behavior, help them learn to unconditionally *forgive* that behavior, while at the same time challenging them to change it. And most important: help them dive into the emptiness that underlies all this extreme behavior.

There is hope for recovery, and just like with an alcoholic, it comes from the sufferer deciding: *"This is a serious problem,"* not *"I'm special."* Yes, people should feel safe and not judged in seeking out mental health counseling. But demanding that others perceive your disorder in a certain way is a losing battle, which only serves to distract you from recovery. Romanticizing this is akin to telling an alcoholic: *"You're not the problem! If the rest of the world would just accept your drinking, then you'd be fine—you're the true victim here."*

People with BPD have extremely unhealthy attachment patterns that need to be identified and explored, not romanticized. My goal is to help you feel comfortable in your own skin so you can enjoy the company of others, rather than obsessing about their every move. So that you can see them as individual human beings, rather than a solution to everything or a guaranteed source of unconditional love. The idea here is to instead reactivate your own source of unconditional love, from within, so that you do not need to seek it from others.

We cannot do these things when we are focused on controlling everyone else's perception of us. For example, BPD sufferers will often seek out resources and forums meant for folks recovering from a BPD ex or loved one. Then the person with BPD will read stories and feel victimized, as if the writers are attacking *them* personally. This is all the protective self trying to find new ways to feel devastated and persecuted—almost like a form of self-harm.

And by the way, this is a two-way street! Partners of people with BPD might also visit online forums meant for people with BPD, and angrily comment to posters, lecturing them as if they are speaking to their own partner. So we need to shift our perspective from a persecution competition to a recognition that both "sides" are hurting.

The way I see it, if you're doing well and recovering, it doesn't really matter what people say about people with untreated BPD. The truth is they can be really difficult, challenging, and even abusive. That's why the stigma exists. The solution is not to try to control what people on the Internet think of other people (this is an impossible task, and therefore not a fun one). The solution is to focus on yourself and be happy with your own recovery, so that it does not feel like a personal attack on *you* when other people vent about *their* own exes or parents.

People will probably continue to complain about how their exes or parents with BPD are monsters until the end of time. The real question is: Are you a monster? If not, great! That means their complaints have nothing to do with you. Put the healthy boundaries you've established to good use by not getting triggered and taking these comments personally.

We will find no peace trying to control others; we can only control ourselves. Be the change you want to see. Be an awesome partner, friend, or family member who happens to have BPD.

Conversation with Linda

I met Linda through a BPD community on Reddit. She bonds with others by sharing stories of trauma from her childhood, seeking out sympathy and comfort from anyone who will offer it. She has a great boyfriend but she's terrified that he might leave her at any time. She needs constant reassurance that she is sexy and loved and needed. But even when he gives her this reassurance, she feels a nagging discomfort—a sense of emptiness—so she assumes something is wrong.

"Are you noticing the feeling of emptiness today?" I asked.

She burst into tears, the same way she often began our conversations. "I can't stand Roger!" she said. "He's starting to remind me of every other guy I've dated."

"I'm sorry to hear that. What happened?"

"He takes such a long time to reply to texts," she said. "I know he's busy with work, but when I don't hear back, I assume he's angry or planning to leave me. I can't believe he's pulling this crap. He seemed so much different than Charlie and Andrew at first, but now he's even worse."

"How are you doing now?"

"Not that bad, actually!" she said. Her mood seemed to have shifted and the crying stopped. "Also, I'm really proud of myself. After I finish talking with you, I've decided I'm going to go shopping and buy some new clothes."

"I thought you were trying to stay in control of your credit card debt?"

Her voice became louder. "I actually talked with my boss and aunt about this, and they're both really good with money. They agreed I need to live for myself, and not let finances control my life. I deserve to feel pretty after everything that happened in my childhood, you know?"

"I agree you deserve to feel pretty," I said. "I just want to make sure you won't later regret spending the money."

"Yeah, I'm starting to realize I never gave myself the opportunity to be pretty when I was younger," she said. "I've been journaling about my past, and I'm remembering a lot of things I blocked out. Kids used to bully me, scream at me, and call me fat."

"Wow, that must have been very painful," I said. "What about the emptiness? Have you had a chance to explore that?"

"Well, I've been uncovering a lot of trauma." Her eyes were brimming with tears again. "I'm realizing people have always hated me."

"But what about the *sensation* of emptiness?" I persisted, trying to steer the conversation away from the stories and back to her bodily sensations. "What does that feel like in your body?"

"I don't know," she said impatiently. "It's just sort of numb and disconnected, I can't describe it. That's not the problem anyway. Like I was saying before, the problem is that other people have always hated me."

Linda's homework: Take a step back from sharing trauma stories and romanticizing others as the "solution" to your happiness. Do not seek sympathy or attention to make you feel good. Do not engage in shopping sprees or other impulsive behavior. Instead, sit with the uncomfortable feelings of emptiness.

Other Protective Selves

Wounds and their resulting protective selves can be very complex. I've identified some of the most common ones in the previous sections, but certainly there are many other variations and combinations. My goal with this book is to resonate with any reader, specific to their own unique experiences, so I've outlined a few other brief examples below. If any of them resonate with you, you can apply all of the practices and suggestions throughout the rest of the book. While protective selves may differ in their manifestations, the general foundation is identical: core wound, protective self, and external measures of worth.

- Workaholic: Some people shine through their work, and that's totally fine. The problem with the protective self is when it becomes a distraction tool from ever exploring your inner world. If you feel empty or numb and find yourself voluntarily working late hours and weekends, this may be a sign that you're not really running the show. Workaholics tend to wear their protective self like a badge of honor, using their work as a primary measure of their self-worth. Similar to the perfectionist, you may find yourself surrounded by unending self-imposed projects and ideas, adding more and more to your plate so you never have a chance to slow down. Your protective self will scoff at the idea that you should find more balance in your work life, because it wants you to keep obsessing over your work. That way you don't have to explore the discomfort in your body. To begin healing, workaholics will have to start making some pretty major changes to their daily lives and priorities.

- Narcissistic Personality Disorder: I hesitated about including narcissists in this book, because I know it could cause some discomfort for survivors of cluster-B relationships. Abuse survivors often cling to these relationships in hopes that the person can change, and my goal here is actually to encourage the opposite. You cannot fix or change another person. No external source of love or compassion can change this person. It has to come from within. The narcissistic protective self is obsessed with attention, image, and winning. The protective self does not experience shame or remorse, because those things are numbed away in the body. They are often described as "heartless" and this may be because their own hearts feel like they are "missing." The narcissistic protective self's primary distraction tool is *boredom*. By keeping the narcissist constantly bored, the protective self is always seeking new types of attention or thrills and never slows down to explore its own inner world. The narcissist becomes obsessed with potential new partners, mirroring them and copying their personality so they fall in love, only to eventually become bored when that person offers their love. When narcissists harm their loved ones, they feel that it is justified because the protective self convinces them that those loved ones are bad, and have actually victimized *you*. The protective self is unable to admit fault or wrongdoing, because doing so would be to explore the sensation of shame, and the protective self's entire purpose is to keep you, the narcissist, away from that shame. It can be very difficult to penetrate because it scoffs at the idea of needing help—it sees itself as superior. Even when you try to meditate, it will send you persistent messages of ridicule and derision at what a stupid idea that is. Use your mindfulness to notice that voice. To begin healing, you will need to sit with the sensation of boredom over and over again, and learn how to *not* act on the impulse to relieve that boredom. Use mindfulness to focus especially on sensations in the heart and stomach.

· Paranoid: This type can be especially difficult, because paranoid types believe everything to be a conspiracy or plot. The paranoid protective self will likely even react that way to reading these sentences. Paranoid types usually feel a deep inner agitation, and so their protective self keeps them externally focused on grand schemes and conspiracy theories. Someone is always out to get them, keep them down, or manipulate them. Even where there may be much simpler explanations, they will go down complex rabbit holes to explain everything. For example, you might get a password reset notification from Facebook that you did not request. Instead of assuming it to be a spammer or phishing attempt, you decide that the government is trying to log in to your profile because you know too much. Even though recent leaks would indicate that the government can view your private information any time they want *without* needing to reset your password, the protective self prefers this grandiose version of events where you are being targeted because you're a threat to the omniscient "them." Anyone who tries to help talk you out of this will be seen as part of the conspiracy. The protective self reinforces itself by being somewhat aggressive, hostile, and cold—then when people react negatively to this, the protective self can prove that people are not to be trusted. Paranoid types have often been betrayed or mistreated, and their bodies have adopted this rigid sensation and corresponding stories in order to protect them from that pain. Paranoid types can find peace when they stop waging these external battles, and instead turn their attention inward. When they realize that their bodies and minds are only trying to protect them, this naturally begins to soften the heart (along with all of the anxious thinking patterns).

· Blamer: People who blame everyone else for the problems in their life often have the most ironic wound of all. They secretly believe they are to blame for everything. But this wound is buried so far away that the protective self doesn't even experience it. It just constantly looks externally for people doing them wrong. Blamers freely offer criticisms about everyone else, but react quite badly when confronted with criticism themselves. They'll judge or insult others, but a minor disagreement from anyone else is seen as an assault on their entire identity. They may have a puffed-up image of themselves that pretends to love criticism, but when genuine arguments occur, they become extremely defensive, accusatory, and dismissive. They'll accuse the other person of being "hysterical" or "hypersensitive," while they themselves are the one exhibiting this quality. They use manipulation and blame to turn the conversation back on the other person. It is particularly difficult to get through this protective self, because it is projecting so many of its own faults onto other people. It cannot admit fault or even entertain these ideas, because that would take them down the dark path toward their wound. Even when proven to be false, the blamer cannot take responsibility or apologize. To any onlooker, it almost seems silly what lengths they go to in order to avoid admitting fault. To approach healing, blamers will need to turn their focus away from these external stories of blame and keep their attention on the difficult sensations that arise when they're not obsessing over other people. The protective self has kept blamers distracted with thinking about other people because it does not want them to dive inside where the pain lives. But as a blamer, you can make this leap, and I promise it will not consume you.

There are many other protective selves out there, and as you begin this hard work on yourself, it'll become much easier to identify your own unique tendencies and distractions. I've used labels and psychological terms to help put symptoms into various buckets, but from this point forward, don't worry too much about the labels. They are helpful for learning about your current state of mind, but from here on out, they aren't going to have much more meaning—because the labels are not who you actually are.

The labels are not who you actually are.

PART 3

Deconstructing the Protective Self

In order to make any progress with the underlying wound, we first need to deconstruct the protective self. Otherwise our healing will still be done through the controlling and distracting lens of the protective self, and we will find ourselves looping in circles. The protective self encourages this infinite loop so that it can remain in control. It keeps you on a completely different emotional "wavelength" from the pain. In order to return to that wavelength, we must be willing to slow down our lives, distractions, and thought processes.

Imagine you're listening to the same radio station every day. Just because you're listening to that radio station doesn't mean it's the only station playing music, right? It just so happens to be the one station—the one wavelength—that you're tuned in to. But if you wanted to, you could change the station and you'd hear different music. And that other music has been there all along, despite your not listening to it.

Emotional wounds are a lot like that. You're listening to one radio station, then you experience some type of trauma. To protect you, your mind switches to another radio station. The problem is, the pain still exists on your old radio station. So your mind tricks you into listening to the new station, over and over again. That way you'll always stay distracted from the pain.

It's not even a conscious choice, so there's no point in judging or blaming yourself. With trauma, your mind and body make decisions for you. You might think you're running the show, but you're not. Instead, you're given an infinite list of distractions to keep you tuned in to the "safe" wavelength, to give you the illusion of control. The protective self's promise is: *"If [external thing] just happens, then you will feel better."* This is the trick of the protective self, and it will keep you hungering for external measures of worth until you take back control in order to heal for good.

You wouldn't expect an alcoholic to make much recovery progress while still drinking alcohol. Likewise, you can't expect to make progress while you're still relying on external measures of worth.

In my protective self's heyday, life was all about accomplishments: taking on new projects, writing more books, anything to keep my mind going a million miles an hour. Even when I wasn't working on them, I'd put on my headphones and blast music to fantasize about them. To imagine how good it would feel once I finished, and how others would hopefully enjoy them too.

At one point, I was juggling a full-time job, writing my

third book, and coordinating a mass migration to a new website software for a forum with millions of visitors. The migration involved hundreds of hours of technical work, perfecting every little detail to make sure the transition went smoothly. And it did. We went live without a hitch, people loved the new website. They loved it so much that we went from seeing two hundred new posts per day to two thousand. It shot up in the Google rankings too, bringing on more members than ever before. Mission accomplished!

Except for some reason, I felt worse. The numb feeling in my heart wasn't getting any better, even though I got exactly what I had fantasized about.

On top of that, the website now required *more* attention, because there were dozens of reports and conflicts every single day. And I hated conflict. Why had I willingly dug myself into more of it? Every day was spent dealing with accusations, conspiracies, drama, and anger. Negotiating peace between full-grown adults while I had no peace of my own. The larger the website grew, the more drama it created.

If you're thinking there's an obvious solution here, don't worry, I'll get there in about a year.

Instead, I decided I needed to upgrade our servers and create *more* plug-ins to help moderate the website. I started piecing together an elaborate transition plan that would take hundreds more hours to complete. At the same time, another recovery website asked me to help moderate their community, which I enthusiastically agreed to. Additionally, I thought we should start a non-profit organization to help us raise awareness and attract *more* readers. Becoming a CEO, of course, was exactly what I needed in my life. The missing piece of my happiness puzzle. Sure . . .

It's sort of funny in hindsight, but you can see how my thinking was actually quite unhealthy, right? And that's why we need to *stop* feeding the protective self, or it will keep going down the same path forever. It will happily keep you distracted and obsessing about the past and future so that you are never in the present moment. So you never slow down enough to experience the truth in your body. Of course, the irony is that only by experiencing it can you finally release it and move on.

What the protective self *wants* is in direct conflict with what you *need*. Albert Einstein said something to the effect that we can't seek to solve problems within the same mind-set that created them. In this case, the mind-set *is* the problem, so we're definitely not going to have much luck solving it with our mind.

After starting the non-profit and changing the servers, I eventually had a nervous breakdown. It seemed like a curse at the time. How could life be so unfair? I was doing everything right! But it turned out to be the first good thing that had happened to me in a very long time.

I started dialing way back on the accomplishments. No more writing for a while. We closed down the website, disabled new registrations, and began dissolving the non-profit. When I got the urge to fantasize about a new project, I used mindfulness to quell those thoughts.

As all of this was happening, the feeling in my heart got

so much worse. Again, it felt unfair. I was doing all the right things. Why was I feeling *worse*?

Because without my old external measures of worth, my protective self was crumbling. As the protective self dies, the underlying wound exposes itself. And it doesn't feel good.

As long as you feel any form of numbness, your protective self is still in charge. You are stuck in distraction mode. This is why I spend little time discussing stories when someone describes feeling "emptiness" or "tightness" or "boredom." As long as those things exist, I'm just talking to (and feeding) the protective self. We're getting nowhere. So in order to get started, we must first deconstruct the protective self.

Once it's gone, it's gone. There's no going back to the protective self, even if you want to. As horrible as this might feel at first, it's actually a really *good* thing. Because once you are reintroduced to your wound, then true healing can begin. You can finally make progress after so many years of running in circles.

The key is, you have to be ready to embrace whatever happens when your protective self fails. Remember, it offered a temporary solution to a problem long ago when you did not know how to fix it. The body doesn't do this unless it deems those problems intolerable and detrimental to your own survival. And so it's safe to assume this is not going to be a pleasant experience.

Once the wound starts coming out, it's common to face overwhelming fears that you're crazy, you're awful, you're doing it all wrong, you're hopeless, you're ruining everything, you're a liar . . . But you will eventually have an "ah-hah" moment where you realize that's the *exact* sensation your body has been trying to keep you away from for so long.

If you can meet *that* sensation with mindfulness and unconditional love, you can finally stay with the discomfort that your body tried to numb away. Then there is no more need for numbness or the protective self, because you are able to stay with the pain, *without acting on it or believing it.*

So how do we get to that point?

The protective self, while complicated, is also surprisingly predictable. The following sections will help you deconstruct the protective self so you can finally feel the wound that it hides from you—and begin to truly heal.

Beyond Numbness

Underneath the protective self is an uncomfortable, indescribable feeling: numb, void, blocked up, hollow, tight, empty, or bored. Stephen Wolinsky refers to it as a "layer of amnesia," and it's exactly what your protective self serves to maintain. Believe it or not, that numbness is where the true self is stored. But how are you supposed to get in touch with "numbness"? It's extremely frustrating, because even though you may wish to help yourself, you can't. And it's not your fault.

With emotional trauma, people are often (unknowingly) cut off from their own emotions, in order to protect them from the sheer intensity of the pain. This is especially true with toxic shame, which is such a self-destructive state of mind that the body actually "disables" it (along with many other emotions) in order to stop the chaos and make you functional. Emotions are stored in the body, so trauma splits you away from that part of yourself. This can feel hopeless, like you're permanently damaged and unable to feel emotions normally. However, recognizing this issue is actually the first step toward approaching your trauma from a gentle and caring perspective.

Allow the numbness to be there, and understand that it wouldn't be there unless it was protecting you from some extremely overwhelming stuff. That's the key step toward working beyond numbness: understanding that it shot up as a defense to protect you, because you simply were not able to cope with the emotions at the time. Knowing that your body and spirit did these things for your body paradoxically helps you soften your body.

This numbness is holding some very deep and very difficult wounds. It is refusing to let you back in because it's afraid of returning to that place. The problem is, that's also where your love is stored. If you want your love, you'll need to go back inside to find it. You need to understand that numbness only occurs when there is an intolerable amount of pain: rejection, shame, guilt, self-loathing, self-doubt, and fear. Our bodies are built for survival, and at some point your body decided that these feelings were detrimental to your survival.

Here is the common starting place: "What nonsense. I'm totally fine except for this feeling of boredom!" or "I have no issues except that tight feeling in my heart" or "I am completely functional except for that constant void in my stomach."

And this is exactly my point. You don't even feel this pain

because your body is preventing you from experiencing it. This is one of the biggest challenges with these issues, because sufferers (understandably) believe they are totally and completely fine aside from that vague numbness.

But being unable to feel your heart, or feeling a void in your stomach or a black hole you can't describe, or feeling dead inside or constant boredom . . . these are signs of damage. Especially when you examine your corresponding behaviors, you start to realize that there is much more going on than "just that numb feeling." Remember, the protective self is *always* trying to convince you that there's nothing wrong, to keep you from experiencing the unbearable sensation that *everything is wrong.*

Approaching this from another perspective, imagine your body as a highway. At some point in your life, there was a crash on the highway. Not just a little crash, but a fifty-car pileup. Unsure how to clean up the mess, the police decided to block off that part of the highway and reroute traffic off at a previous exit, then back onto the highway a few miles after the crash. It's not the most efficient route—requires more gas, takes more time— but it gets you to your destination safely.

Any time you check to see if the highway route is available yet, you're met by police officers who won't let you in. They're friendly but firm, and they route you to the detour instead. You never even get a glimpse of the wreckage. With time, you forget there was even a car crash. The detour starts to feel normal. You don't even bother checking on the highway route anymore.

But as time passes, the detour becomes more and more congested. It wasn't designed to take on all of the traffic from the highway. Everyone's wasting gas and time trying to get to their destination in a very inefficient way. Drivers are getting irritable and frustrated. Crashes become more frequent. People are late to work.

Until one day, it's so unbearable that you finally return to the highway and demand to see what's going on at the crash site. The police refuse, despite your every effort to get back in. You start to wonder, what the heck is going on in there? How have they not cleaned up the crash after so many years?

In a way, this is what your body does to protect you from emotional trauma and shame. It doesn't yet have the tools to heal those things, so it numbs them, pushes them away in your body, and routes you around them. In this process, some parts of your mind and body become overused to make up for the deficiency in the area that's been blocked off.

It's not like you're consciously aware that this is happening, and it's certainly not like you asked for it. It was a decision made *for* you, by your body. Even if you try to get back in, it won't let you. So if you're harboring any self-blame or embarrassment, please let that go right now. You can't possibly remain upset with yourself for something you didn't do.

And the good news is, there are ways back inside.

To begin this work, meditate on the numbness and ask your body to allow you to experience those feelings. Ask it over and over again. You want to feel reconnected to your body again. This is one of the most frustrating parts of the process, because you'll likely just be met with more numbness. Eventually you may become so frustrated that you yell out loud or break down, begging your body to let you in.

This process is essential for developing your unconditional love (from the Tools section). Watch your frustration, see yourself trying to get back in. Regard yourself with kindness, see how hard you are trying.

Do not try to label or analyze the sensations. This is especially common in therapy when patients may think they are "supposed" to feel a certain emotion. If all you feel is dull numbness, then that's all you feel, and that's fine. *Do not try to tell yourself a story about the sensation* ("Underneath this numbness must be my sadness about my mother not loving me!"). You cannot "think" your way into feeling. This is actually about *slowing down* your thinking, so you can get on the same wavelength as your body.

As you begin to accept the numbness as it is, you form a stronger relationship with your body. You are no longer at war with it, but rather genuinely interested in hearing its message. And even if it refuses to share that message with you, you're still willing to stay with it. You might grow frustrated and impatient every once in a while, but that's okay. You can recognize that too, and accept how frustrating it is to be locked out of your own body.

Eventually this leads to the most important question of all: Who is this part of you noticing that you're trying to get back in touch with your body?

Throughout the rest of the book, we'll check in with each of the conversations from Part 2, to see how their protective self experiences topics like numbness, resentment, triggers, fear, and shame.

Avoidant and Numbness

"Can you think of any other words to describe the tightness?" my therapist asked me.

"No," I said. "That's what's so frustrating. I've been at this for so long and no one knows what it could be. It's just always *tight*."

"Does it feel good or bad?"

"I don't know. It just doesn't feel . . . right," I said. "Like I know it's not supposed to be there. But it doesn't feel particularly bad. Like I said, there aren't any emotions associated with it. It's just a physical sensation."

"Have you ever tried communicating with it? Asking it questions?"

"Yes," I said, frustrated. "I've tried everything. Nothing ever changes. It's just the same tightness, over and over again."

"Can you tell me what happens when you try to communicate with it?"

"Well, I imagine the tightness as a little boy hugging my heart," I said. "I ask him why he's there. He says he's just trying to protect me."

"That's really nice you've got someone looking out for you!"

"Yeah, and I've asked him numerous times to try hugging a little less hard—even for just a minute."

"Does anything happen?"

"Nope. Never any difference," I said. "So do you have any idea what this could be? Or am I just stuck with it forever?"

"Hmm . . . Well, I think you're being blocked."

"What?"

"I think your mind and body are working together to keep you out," she said. "I think your heart has been numbed out, because it's carrying some extremely difficult emotions."

"But I already told you, it's just physical. No bad emotions or anything like that. I'm a pretty cheerful guy otherwise."

"In the novel you're writing, you described characters dealing with inadequacy, rage, shame, self-doubt, judgment, and rejection. Those don't sound very cheerful!"

"I don't know where those characters came from," I said. "But I haven't felt those things myself."

"Those would be very normal things to feel after what you went through—abuse, infidelity, and shame. What if parts of your body are trying to express themselves through your characters, even if you're not feeling them yourself right now?"

"I don't get it," I said. "How is it possible for me to have feelings stored in my own body that I can't even feel?"

"Trauma works in interesting ways to protect us," she said. "With that perspective, you can almost begin to see it in a sympathetic light."

"So then how do I get back in touch with my feelings? Do I need to ask the little boy?"

"Actually, I think the boy is the one keeping you *away* from your feelings."

"By hugging me?" I asked skeptically.

"No, the entire idea of the boy," she said. "I think that is some part of your brain trying to keep you out. Masking complex emotions and real suffering with the projection of an imaginary boy protecting you."

"So how else am I supposed to communicate with my tightness?"

"Look at how hard your body and mind are working to protect you," she said. "I think that fact alone will start to soften your heart so you can see what's in there."

"Okay," I said, determined. "Should I stop listening to music too?"

"Why would you do that?"

"Well, I mean, when I listen to the music I get into that *high* mode where I'm imagining my stories and characters. If I'm supposed to cut down the distractions, shouldn't I stop doing that?"

"Your imagination's activation with music is a great gift," she said. "Please don't stifle your imagination. Instead, you just need to redirect it."

"How?"

"In the past, you used music and imagination to get lost in these fantasy worlds of your own characters and ideal future scenarios. So now you can still use music and imagination, but use it on yourself instead. You like the idea of unconditional love, right?"

"Yes."

"Okay, so try imagining that love being offered to you—in your body—in the present moment. Rather than a far-off fantasy."

"Okay, yeah, I can do that."

"Good. But as you do this, be prepared for some very difficult emotions to surface."

"That's totally fine," I said excitedly. "That's *good*! I would rather feel bad feelings than numbness."

BPD and Numbness

"I'm starting to realize that I'm just not meant for this world," Linda said. "I have so much love to offer, but no one wants it."

"Linda, can I be honest with you for a minute?"

She looked taken aback. "Okay . . ."

"If we're going to make any progress here, I need you to focus on shifting from the story to your body. You have a lot of difficult stories, and I fully respect how hard they must be for you. However, this type of healing is actually about pausing the stories and focusing on the body."

"What do you mean?"

"The emptiness in your body," I said. "I think these stories are keeping you away from it."

"Here we go again with the emptiness." She rolled her eyes. "I had so much I wanted to talk about today, and you're still stuck on the emptiness. You know, the emptiness is probably there *because* of all these bad things that keep happening to me."

"And I'm not denying that possibility," I said. "All I'm asking is that you take a few minutes right now to focus on the emptiness in your body and see what happens."

She nodded and closed her eyes. Within moments, she was sobbing again and telling stories about her abusive mother, convinced that's what her emptiness must be hiding.

Once again, I gently interrupted her. "Linda, the stories work you up into a frenzy, *thinking* your way into extreme emotions that actually make it difficult to focus on the emptiness. The emptiness isn't going to reveal itself in just two minutes by recalling a childhood memory."

"Jesus Christ, I'm trying!"

"I know," I said. "But—"

"This is so invalidating. It's just like my abusive mom, honestly. I'm trying to share a story and you just keep changing the subject. She was always invalidating me."

"Linda, I could offer you all the validation in the world, but I care for you, and I want you to feel better. I don't think external validation is the key to feeling better. I want you to feel happy on your own, without my validation."

"You do?"

"Yes!" I said. "But I don't need you to strive for any sort of result or breakthrough. I just want you to try focusing only on your body and staying with whatever comes up. If you notice your brain jumping to stories about childhood, don't get mad at yourself. Just kindly notice it, rather than getting caught up in the corresponding emotions."

She nodded again. "Okay."

After a few minutes of silence, she looked up.

"How did it go?" I asked. "Did you notice any particular sensations in your body?"

"I guess," she said. "The emptiness is in my stomach and my head. Just this empty void. And I have no idea what it is, or where it came from. It's mind-numbingly boring."

"Awesome."

"Awesome?" She laughed. "What am I supposed to do with that?"

"Just keep doing that meditation whenever you can. Especially when you notice the distracting stories come up. Just tell yourself, 'Hey, it's the stories again!' and work on shifting the focus back to your emptiness."

"Emptiness, emptiness, emptiness." She smiled. "God, you're annoying."

"Yes," I agreed.

External to Internal

One of the biggest challenges with the protective self is that it tricks you into focusing all of your energy externally. Numbing sensations like boredom and emptiness convince you to do something to *relieve* that boredom. It's actually a very clever ploy by the protective self. The same is true for workaholics, who constantly get new "ideas" for big projects to take on. Or codependents, who become consumed with the idea of "helping" others. Or people with BPD, who are prey to a constant stream of tragic stories and impulsive behaviors. The protective self is always bombarding you with new and tempting distractions.

But with mindfulness and daily practice, we can learn to

Mindfulness/Unconditional Love

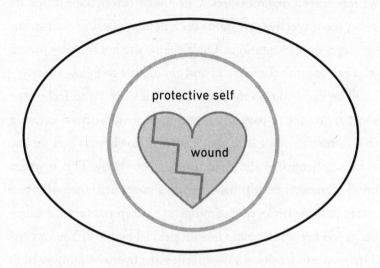

start declining that external focus. If we get the overwhelming sensation to "do" something, we can notice that sensation and decline it. As soon as we begin *noticing* the tricks of the protective self, they actually become pretty transparent.

So for the next step in our diagram, we're going to remove "external measures of worth," and suddenly we're left not feeling so great.

When we decline external distractions, the alternative is to focus on our internal experience. As mentioned in the previous section, this can be very frustrating because sometimes the best description a person can find for their internal experience is "numbness" or "tension." What are you supposed to do with that?

And that's exactly the problem. All of this external focus has caused us to accidentally abandon what's really going on inside us. Without knowing our own internal emotions and feelings, we rely on external measures. Once those external measures are gone, the protective self fights back harder, offering even stronger urges and temptations. Once again, you are the *only* person who can identify these tricks and choose not to follow them.

The more you do this, the *worse* you're going to feel in the short term. You're basically stopping your mind from entering this distraction overdrive mode, which slowly puts you on the same wavelength as the discomfort in your body. This is where non-judgmental mindfulness makes a huge difference. If you're aware of these tricks your mind plays to keep you focused externally, you become less and less influenced by them. You can endure pain and tension without feeling the overwhelming need to distract yourself from it. And if you do find yourself focused externally, you can gently bring your attention back to your body, helping to form new habits.

In *Psychopath Free*, I wrote about the idea of a "constant." A constant is someone you can rely on, who always inspires and never disappoints. Someone you can use as a baseline to compare and understand when someone is not treating you well. It sounded really nice to me at the time, but the problem with the whole idea is that it's externally focused. It's relying on another human being to be a perfect source of unconditional love, and then wondering why nobody seems to meet this impossible standard.

Looking back, I think the idea of a constant is one of the protective self's greatest desires and distractions. It keeps you constantly searching *externally* to set your *internal* gauge. This is a recipe for unhappiness because you are always looking to others for love and consistency, when no human being can offer this 100 percent of the time. It's using a person in place of our own intuition, and keeping us hinged on the reactions of others.

Cluster-B Abuse Survivor and Internal Focus

Often after narcissistic abuse, survivors feel that they've lost a part of themselves: love and joy. They worry that they'll never be the same person again, as if that old person is lost and gone forever. But this is simply not true. We can always restore that part of ourselves, but we can't do it when we're focusing all our energy on the person who abused us. As long as we believe a part of us has been "stolen," we are distracted from the very tools needed to heal it.

Recovery comes from experiencing the pain fully, rather than trying to pretend we're fine or happy. And with cluster-B relationships, it's not just the typical pain of a breakup or being mistreated. It's the pain of being separated from love in such a traumatic, unexpected way. When a trusted loved one abandons or rejects us the way cluster-B disordered individuals do, our bodies tend to absorb a message of inner defectiveness: *"This person rejected or abused me because something is very bad about me."*

While you may logically understand this isn't true, the body is not so easy to convince. Living in there are often deep feelings of self-doubt, inadequacy, worthlessness, and rejection. As we allow ourselves to experience those things, we get in touch with the truest parts of who we are, no matter how intolerable those feelings might be. Our most vulnerable, authentic self was shamed and humiliated away from conscious awareness. But we can find it again, in our bodies.

In the end, it's not really about what the other person did, but the messages they left behind in you, which stay there regardless of any external factors.

Cluster-B disordered individuals often give the target a "spotlight" effect—like all the attention and focus of the world is on you. This comes from the love-bombing, flattery, constant communication, grandiosity, and personality mirroring. Basically, a completely inappropriate amount of attention, but it *feels* good.

All of this allows us to slip from internal measures of worth to external ones. This person thinks so highly of us, puts us on a pedestal above everyone else. It's easy to hang on to their every word, because it feels so good.

But once they split to devaluation, the opposite happens. They start to lie and triangulate with others. Because our worth is invested in them, we become obsessed with proving ourselves and trying to win back our place as "number one." Our focus becomes more external, waiting (even begging) for their next communication like a drug.

Then the discard happens and they immediately replace us with someone else. Our focus becomes even *more* external. How is the new couple so happy? Who is this person they chose over you? Why are they better than you? Why do they get better treatment than you?

External focus becomes external obsession, trying to prove

we're happy too. Consumed by resentment and revenge fantasies, imagining how much better we'd feel if their lives were ruined, or their new relationship came crumbling down. It's this sort of manic, delusional energy that appears unstable to onlookers.

With time, things calm down, but the focus is often still stuck in "external." Perfectionism, staying busy, caretaking, being overly nice, seeking approval, impulsive behaviors, grandiosity, vengeful or resentful thoughts, and even addiction. These are all temporary bursts of external worth. Often this becomes so serious that mental illness forms: C-PTSD, avoidant personality, codependency, and even borderline personality.

The problem is, our focus is still stuck externally. In order to heal, we need to turn the focus inside ourselves. So it becomes less about "this person did awful things to me" and more about "this is how I feel right now on the inside, independent of external factors."

With both Mel and Elliot, we had to spend a lot of time noticing how much rumination was really going on. There were so many stories, so much (understandable) frustration, and such strong feelings of unfairness and betrayal. Mel had developed an intent focus on psychopathy, to the point where she had very little time to focus on herself. Everything in her life, even politics and creativity, had become about psychopathy. As someone who had been there myself, I could only offer Mel my personal experience that shifting our thoughts—away from psychopathy, toward our bodies—can start to yield really important changes.

On a different (but similar) note, Elliot was still so preoccupied with his borderline girlfriend's problems that he had almost no understanding of his own emotions, beyond the fact that he was frustrated at his girlfriend (which was, again, about her). But with some reflection, he was able to start noticing this pattern where her crisis stories never seemed to get better, and therefore his expectation of improvement was unrealistic. If he couldn't save her, could he at least build a stronger relationship with himself?

The reason internal focus is so important is that we are the only people who can do the hard work to release these old messages and reconnect ourselves with love.

Perfectionist and Internal Focus

The perfectionist's life is all about external focus. Sarah was so stuck on her accomplishments and successes that it became physically uncomfortable to sit still. It was like her mind moved a million miles an hour, even when she was supposed to be relaxing.

"I don't even know how to slow down," said Sarah. "If I slow down, then I will lose everything I've worked for."

"That is the protective self talking," I said. "It hangs on to this manufactured world for dear life, convincing you that if you stop giving it your full attention, something terrible will happen. What's the worst that could happen if you eased up on all your hard work?"

"I'd fall behind," she said. "I'd never be able to catch back up."

"Well, you'd never be able to catch back up to your current pace. But I don't exactly see you suddenly doing nothing with your life and becoming a gigantic failure. You don't seem like the type."

She smiled. "So you just think I should slow down the pace a little?"

"I think it would be really good for you, so you can have some time to explore your own inner world, rather than the one you've built outside—although I admit it's impressive."

"Okay," she said. "I think I can do that. And what should I expect to start happening?"

"Well, to be honest, I think you're going to start feeling pretty bad."

She laughed. "Way to sell it, Jackson!"

"I know, I know. I just want to be realistic that without all of your external distractions, your body may start to reveal some pretty difficult stuff."

"And what should I do when it does?"

"Just stay with it," I said. "Your immediate impulse is going to be to find another project or accomplishment to focus on. I guarantee it. So if you can *notice* that impulse and pleasantly decline it, you'll start to make some great progress."

"I think I can do that. But I have to ask, what's the point of all this? Why make myself feel bad?"

"Because once you feel the badness, you can work on a new type of solution—one that doesn't involve external distractions."

"But my distractions work okay."

"Yes, but imagine if you didn't have to try so hard. Imagine if you could just feel light and free in your own body, without being surrounded by any accomplishment."

She sighed. "That sounds like bliss."

Resentment

*Anger is a powerful and sometimes frightening
emotion. It's also a beneficial one if it's not allowed to
harden into resentment or used as a battering ram to
punish or abuse people.*

—MELODY BEATTIE

Almost any spiritual or psychological guide will outline the reasons why resentment is unhealthy for the body, mind, and heart. Even years after the abuse has ended, a person can "move on" (never consciously thinking about the abuser anymore) while still carrying resentment in the body. This can start to manifest in numerous different ways: depression, anxiety, addiction, irritability, blood pressure problems, and changes in energy levels.

While most of the disorders in this book stem from betrayal and abuse, a lot of this journey is actually about *releasing* the idea of betrayal from our own hearts, so that we can be free. Betrayal convinces us that we are being let down, and that our needs won't be met. Breaking beyond this belief (however true it might have been) allows us to live in the present moment again. This isn't about rewriting history, but rather finding joy and meaning in the process of opening our own hearts.

When working with personality disorders (and the people they hurt), the biggest problem with resentment is that it tightens the lock of the protective self. It keeps us away from the wound. As long as we focus on "bad other," we are distracted from the pain of "bad self." This is not a conscious distraction. It's not like we go home thinking, "Wow, I feel terrible right now, so I'm going to resent someone instead." It's the other way around. The manic, obsessive energy of resentment keeps us in a "high" state, which makes it difficult to feel our own pain. Instead, our pain just becomes a vague numbness.

It's not that the person didn't do anything wrong. It's that hating and focusing on them blocks *you* from the mind-set and tools needed to find love for yourself. As long as we believe "something bad happened to me," we are distracted from the energy that fills us with love.

Grandiosity often follows, and it's just another version of this distracting "high" energy. By imagining big, sweeping things about ourselves and our future, we are on an entirely different wavelength from our bodies. Our minds have taken control to *keep us out* of our bodies in the present moment. Narcissists envision unlimited success, power, or admiration. Their victims often fantasize about revenge and justice.

Basically, our minds convince us if these things happen, we'll be happy. Of course this is not true, and we can waste a lifetime chasing that high.

Resentment is the natural reaction to betrayal and pain, so please do not judge yourself for carrying it. The key is discovering what lives behind the resentment. *We don't resent people unless there was a great deal of pain involved.* If a random stranger insults you on the sidewalk, you don't spend months or years ruminating about it. You only do that when you feel hurt or betrayed by someone you love, trust, and care for.

So what specifically did this person hurt? Don't focus on their hurtful behavior, but instead the feelings it brought out in you.

You cannot release resentment with your mind. You cannot *think* your way out of this problem. Instead, you need to gain the tool you don't have: Soothing. Love. The same goes for every single feeling that comes up in this book: self-doubt, worthlessness, guilt. Telling yourself *not* to feel these things will make them feel worse.

A lot of times—and I see this especially with avoidants, perfectionists, C-PTSD, codependents, and borderlines—people reject the idea that they're resentful. They present a happy, calm face to the world and are eternally "nice" to everyone. But on the inside they silently dislike people, writhe with envy, or feel betrayed and slighted by life. This *is* resentment, and we can't make progress if we're just pretending we don't feel it.

What usually happens with a wound is that it's given to you, your body accidentally believes its message, you hate this person, and spend the rest of your life proving you're not what they said you are. Basically you become the *opposite* of your wound. Perfectionists secretly believe they are imperfect and deeply flawed. Codependents secretly believe they are worthless and never enough. Borderlines secretly feel they don't exist, so they are constantly trying to prove their existence (drama, temper, overly emotional). Avoidants secretly believe they have no value, so they find it elsewhere. Sociopaths believe they are powerless, so they seek to dominate and seduce others.

The first key to overcoming resentment is allowing it to be there. Understand that you were thrown into an impossible situation, and you did the best you could at the time. Narcissists and sociopaths cause a great deal of anger in their targets, because they are so intentional and remorseless in their abuse. And they tend to brag about it, which doesn't help. It would be nearly impossible *not* to be resentful about this, so please don't feel any shame or guilt for having a completely normal human reaction to psychological abuse.

Once you've acknowledged and allowed this resentment to be there, the next step is realizing that you might be happier without it. This is not asking you to pretend the abuse wasn't real, or that it wasn't "that bad." It is simply an understanding that your heart might feel more free without resentment, as millions of older and wiser people have already documented long before us.

After that comes the hard part: releasing it. This is a hugely personal path, but several tools that have helped me very much are exploring spirituality, forgiveness (especially of the self), gratitude, and mindfulness. I wasn't a very spiritual person, so this was a slow process for me, but it's also been very rewarding. I learned to be more patient as I discovered this is not an overnight process, but one that takes a lot of time and practice.

Beneath resentment are the real issues: shame, worthlessness, inadequacy, and sadness. When we let down our walls, we're able to work with these softer emotions and realize that our knowledge and intuition still remain fully intact. We do not need to worry about suddenly becoming a doormat again, or bringing another toxic individual into our lives.

In fact, as we explore these underlying wounds, we're likely to start offering something new to ourselves: unconditional love.

When we see someone in pain (including ourselves), this is our natural reaction. And so in this process, tight resentment around the heart is slowly replaced by true love and understanding.

We can use resentment and rumination to develop our unconditional love. It sounds counterintuitive, but it's a great first step. Rumination can be one of the toughest things after a traumatic situation. It serves a purpose for a while (to get you out of the mess and figure out what happened). But eventually it just becomes a bad habit, keeping your mind stuck in obsessive analytical mode and closing off the heart.

Trying to control or stop these thoughts can have the opposite effect, because it just strengthens the same rigid, critical, analytical type of thinking. Meditation can feel frustrating, especially when suffering from trauma, because we're so uncomfortable in our own bodies.

So the next time you're ruminating, try playing the role of a friendly observer who is *watching* you ruminate. You're just listening, interested, and curious. You are not asking yourself to stop, or judging yourself in any way.

So often we think that love is only offered when we are good or think good thoughts, so we try to do everything right all the time and berate ourselves when we stumble. Mindfulness and unconditional love challenge that belief. *Unconditional* means exactly that. You do not have to be "on" all the time. Your anger, resentment, depression, fear, shame, embarrassment—it is all welcomed and cared for.

Every time you start ruminating, just put in a little mental reminder to add in this loving "friend" watching you ruminate.

It's really that simple. With time, that part of you will become automatic. This is the nature of habits. You will eventually start turning to this loving presence, rather than the rumination. It feels so much better in the body, like a soothing medicine, so powerful in washing everything away.

Instead of trying to control or analyze our thoughts (which keeps us in the feedback loop), love activates different parts of our brain and body. The softer vulnerable parts that we often disable after trauma in order to protect ourselves.

This work will also help you discover the parts of yourself that *resist* this love: scream at it, scoff at it, doubt it, fear it. I felt it all around my heart. Remember, all of those parts of you are also welcomed unconditionally.

Codependent and Resentment

"I'm having a lot of trouble with resentment," Tony said. "The other meditations have gone well, but resentment is hard."

"What do you mean?"

"I just realized I've been feeling so used and unappreciated. But then I feel guilty for thinking that, so I just end up feeling bad for thinking negatively about people, which makes me want to try harder to be nice to them."

"Can you give me a specific example of something you resent?"

"Sure," he said. "You know how I help out my best friend with money, right?"

"Yes, I remember that."

"Well, I did that for my ex too, and it went so badly."

"What happened?"

"I literally went broke because of her. She kept telling me sob stories about her job or life situation, making it sound like one more 'big thing' would fix everything. But every time we did that 'big thing,' she became unhappy again. So I helped pay for school, bills, rent, everything. It was never enough. You know how things ended? She cheated on me."

"Wow, I'm so sorry."

"How can you cheat on someone who treats you so well?" He shook his head. "I'm not saying she needs to love me forever, but at least respect me if I'm helping, right?"

"So you resent her for cheating on you after how much you helped her out?"

"Exactly."

"Makes sense to me."

"But I don't want to feel that way!" he said. "She had a difficult past and I just want to forgive her. I don't want to feel resentful."

"Why shouldn't you feel resentful?" I asked. "She did a super-shitty thing."

Tony laughed. "I thought you believed in forgiveness!"

"I do," I said. "But I'm not asking you to be Mother Teresa here. You're allowed to acknowledge when someone does a shitty thing. That's not being unforgiving. It doesn't cause any distress or resentment to say that."

"So what is forgiveness, then? If I'm not understanding her past and feeling sympathy for her, then how do I let go?"

"Forgiveness isn't about digging into her past and feeling sorry for her. It's about learning the lessons from the experience so you don't get hurt that way again. Then you can let go of the resentment and betrayal, because they have nothing else to teach you."

"What am I supposed to learn?"

"Tony, if you can't allow yourself to admit when someone is weird or untrustworthy, you are rejecting your own intuition. You don't need to feel guilty or ashamed for being frustrated with someone. Can you practice allowing that frustration, instead of trying to push it away?"

"I guess . . . ," he said. "It seems so counterintuitive to all of the stuff I've read on forgiveness."

"You don't need to ruminate or plot revenge against her. Just allow your frustration about the situation and listen for messages about *why* you're frustrated."

Tony came back to me a few days later. He had a lot of reasons why he was frustrated.

"I'm frustrated because I think I deserve better. I'm also frustrated at myself because I noticed obvious red flags in her behavior but kept trying to help her because I thought it would fix our relationship. I put up with her nonsense for way longer than I needed to. I am so sick of feeling like I'm never enough for people in my life, but I'm the one who keeps wasting my time on people who are never happy."

"That's great!" I said. "Those are all really, really good messages."

"Really?" He raised his eyebrows. "I think I sound like a whiny brat."

"You don't," I said. "Try acting on some of those thoughts.

Form boundaries, walk away from situations that don't suit you, and walk away faster. You mentioned you're financially supporting your friend, correct?"

"That's right."

"And you said she has an unstable pattern of career changes?"

He smiled. "Yeah, I see where you're going with this."

"Okay, so you have a choice now. You can learn from the past, make smart changes, respect your own needs, and let the resentment go."

"Or . . ."

"Or you can keep doing the same thing over and over again, end up with the short end of the stick, and guarantee you'll feel very resentful down the road."

"Okay, option two it is."

I laughed. "Good call."

"In all seriousness, I will work on this stuff. I'm just worried I'll become bitter and mean to people."

"You discovered some part of you saying 'I matter and I deserve better.' If you start working with that message, I think you'll find the bitterness will subside on its own."

Intentional Triggers

I don't recommend this to people new to recovery, but it's something that I found very helpful later on. I highly recommend doing it in the company of a therapist, because extremely difficult sensations are likely to arise.

The conventional wisdom about triggers is: "This person did X, and therefore they are the reason I feel bad. If they stop doing X, then I will feel okay."

We want to shift toward a new attitude about triggers: "This person did X, which activated a preexisting fear or discomfort inside of me. If I resolve that existing discomfort, then X will not have a significant impact on me."

When we change our definition of triggers, we change our approach to resolving the triggers. With the first view, we are constantly trying to control our surroundings, pad the world, and ensure others behave in a way that doesn't upset us. With the second approach, it's no longer discomfort avoidance, but rather a willingness to explore our own fears and pains so that we can resolve those things, and therefore be left with nothing *to* trigger.

So how can we make this shift?

Start by thinking of somewhere or something you avoid after your traumatic experience. A place, a song, a person, a picture, a memory—anything that you avoid at all costs because it causes great discomfort. Your protective self might trick you by trying to "think" its way into triggers. But the real triggers are the ones that make you *feel* a certain discomfort, typically a sensation that you feel overwhelmingly compelled to act upon. For example, you will likely have *stories* of trauma and abuse that you try to revisit in this practice. However, I'm asking you to look beyond the story and hop back into your body. These are very likely to be moments where you are rejected, humiliated, ignored, patronized, or judged. Situations or memories where you react, contract, or automatically try to change the "channel" in your mind.

This is one of the coolest things, because you start to realize that the moments you feel bad and shrink away from are the *exact* moments I'm trying to get you to lean into. You realize: *"Oh! Wait, it's actually okay that I feel this discomfort."* Not only is it okay—it's the whole point. It's your key back to wholeness.

After my first relationship, I disliked being in the entire city where my ex lived. Fortunately, I didn't need to go there often, but when I did, I always got this indescribable dread. I would try to distract myself and listen to music, fantasizing about some new story. And eventually the feeling would diminish enough for me to forget about it.

One day when I visited the city, I decided to try staying with the feeling. My mind presented lots of memories and stories as to why I felt uncomfortable. I looked at the building where he had been seeing someone else during our actual relationship. So what should that make me feel? Jealousy? Anger? Not really. The sensation behind all of those things was actually something a lot more confusing: inadequacy.

Some part of me had decided that a person cheating on me was a direct result of my not being good enough. Because I was replaced so quickly and effortlessly, I was not enough as I was. There must have been something wrong with me, physically or emotionally. They were better than me. They were superior and I was inferior. It meant that at any given time, a loved one could decide I wasn't enough and replace me with someone else.

Well, that just felt godawful! Instead of realizing none of my old conclusions were true, the inadequacy had stayed inside of me, and I had been desperately trying to disprove it with all of my accomplishments and people pleasing. Nobody can reject me if I'm successful and do everything perfectly, right? Ha.

This is the kind of stuff I'd like for you to explore. With time, you'll start getting excited about the uncomfortable situations, rather than instinctively avoiding them. These feelings can't kill you, they'll just teach you what you need to know about yourself. I want you to adopt a new attitude toward discomfort. Sort of like: *"This feels terrible—and that's a good thing! I have an opportunity to feel it, understand it, and let it go."*

Here are some opportunities to experience this discomfort:

- New date not interested in you
- Person you care about not replying to your text messages
- Feeling shame and dread after a hangover, afraid of how you might have behaved when you weren't in total control
- Old song or photo that reminds you of an ex or loved one who rejected you
- For cluster-B abuse survivors, thinking about the next target who replaced you

So the next time you're rejected after a date, or someone ghosts you, stay with the feeling. Don't act on it. Just be curious and explore it.

As you do this, check with the list of feelings from the

Mindfulness section. For a long time you may not even be aware of what the feeling is, and it might just manifest as a vague anxiety or fear. But eventually it will start to become more and more apparent. Tara Brach and many other Buddhists teach a great mindfulness method called *R.A.I.N.*, which stands for "recognize, allow, investigate, and nonidentification." These steps allow you to *recognize* when a new uncomfortable emotion is experienced, and *allow* that emotion to be experienced (rather than trying to make it go away). The more time you spend *investigating* it with kindness, the more in tune you become with your body, rather than constantly splitting onto a different wavelength. It doesn't feel good, but that is okay, because you are able to start *un-identifying* with it. Yes, it is *real*, but it is not necessarily *true*. And even if it is true, aren't you worthy of a second chance, to let it go so you can experience life without shame?

With mindfulness, you can gently immerse yourself into those situations and allow yourself to explore that discomfort, especially how and where it is felt in your body. The default is just anxiety, which is a jumbled mess of fear saying "avoid this" or "do something." But as we non-judgmentally examine what's behind that discomfort, we're likely to find a lot of the old feelings that our protective selves try very hard to avoid: shame, jealousy, rejection, humiliation, worthlessness, inadequacy, your fault, not enough, or a relentless voice saying "you ruined it and you just need to admit it."

These feelings have nothing to do with the other person anymore. They live inside of you, and you're simply (unknowingly) reacting to an old emotional wound. By developing a kind relationship with yourself, you can slowly agree to experience these feelings fully, staying with them as long as they need (this can take months or even years), before they lose their potency.

Eventually we realize that this is the entire purpose of the protective self: to protect us from ever feeling the same shame or rejection again. But inevitably life continues to throw these situations at us, over and over again, which is why the protective self is *always* destined to fail. Because it is "protecting" us from feeling a part of ourselves that must be released: toxic shame—the belief that we are inherently bad or defective.

The trick is to learn that the shame you feel during your biggest triggers isn't even who you are, so there is nothing to protect you from. If those secret beliefs aren't true, is a life of avoidance really necessary?

The reason your obsessive analytical thoughts exist is to protect you from re-experiencing this shame, so when the shame or rejection happens again, the obsessive thoughts kick into even higher gear. It's an infinite loop! But what if you did the hard work to dig down, feel the shame, and release it? Then your poor mind could finally take a rest and let you be happy.

This is important, so let's look at it another way. Imagine a little girl is rolling around in a field and gets a thorn prick in her side. It hurts a lot, but she doesn't know how to get the thorn out, so she puts a bandage over it.

The next day, her mom hugs her and she recoils in pain. The hug accidentally pushes against the thorn. She decides not to hug anyone anymore, and she goes upstairs to put on a heavy sweater. "There," she says to herself. "That will protect me."

But the next day at recess, she was playing with her friends and fell off the monkey bars. She landed right on her side, and the sweater wasn't enough protection from the thorn. She resolved never to play in the playground again, went home, and put on another sweater.

This continued for months until she wore so many layers of clothes that she looked like an Eskimo in the dead heat of summer. She didn't hug, she didn't play, she didn't do anything. But at least she was safe from the pain.

This is how emotional wounds and shame work. A part of ourselves is hurting, so we keep building protective layer upon layer to avoid the pain. But eventually all those protective layers suffocate us and prevent us from living happy lives. Additionally, they separate us even further from the wound that needs our attention. Triggers seem like a curse at first, because they feel so unpleasant, but in fact, triggers are our key back to the core wound—the thorn—so that we can resolve the thing we're trying to hide.

Triggers are our key back to the core wound.

In the above story, the girl finally takes out the thorn (or asks someone for help). It doesn't feel very good, and it takes a while to heal, but once it's out, there's nothing left to hurt. The next day, she puts on a T-shirt and shorts, hugs her mom, and plays with her friends on the playground.

With time, we realize that triggers are not an attack on our entire being, but it certainly feels that way when we carry hidden shame. The thing is, when we *know who we truly are*—when we've exposed the lie we were fed by the protective self—there aren't really "triggers" anymore, because those beliefs don't live inside of us anymore. There is nothing left *to* trigger. It is much easier to live freely, and to offer your love wherever you wish, especially to yourself.

BPD and Intentional Triggers

"Can you think of an emotional trigger?" I asked Linda.

She laughed. "Only a few hundred. How about the time kids threw food at me during school lunch? Or when I came home and my mom screamed at me for being dirty? Or—"

"These are all very difficult stories," I said. "But I'd like to explore something else, if that's okay with you?"

She looked taken aback. "Okay."

"Last time we talked, you mentioned that Roger takes a long time to reply to your texts."

"Yeah," she said. "But what does that have to do with anything? That's not as traumatizing as my other stories."

"Well, it led you to go on a spending spree," I said. "It triggered an impulsive behavior. So I'm wondering if you can remember what it felt like when you were waiting for his text."

She looked down. "It felt terrible. Like my heart was burning. I thought he wasn't responding because he secretly wanted to break up with me, so I wanted to hurt him first. I was so scared that I even blocked his number for a while so I could feel like I ignored him first."

"That's more like it," I said.

"What?" She looked confused. "It's so stupid. I'm embarrassed that I even care that much about a dumb text message. I can't tell you those things or you'll think I'm insane."

"I don't think that," I said. "I think you've found a *real* trigger. And like most triggers, it gave you an overwhelming urge to *act* on the discomfort you felt in your body. A shopping spree, or really anything to make it go away, right?"

"Yes."

"The next time you feel this same discomfort, I want you to try something different. Instead of acting on it or being afraid of it, just stay with it. And as strange as it sounds, I want you to *welcome* it. I know it feels extremely unpleasant, but it's actually the part of you that needs your attention the most. And it's exposing itself to you. It is your gateway into healing."

"So the next time that awful feeling comes up, I'm just supposed to . . . sit there?"

"Exactly," I said. "Just sit there and notice—with the same love and interest you'd offer to a friend."

"Okay." She nodded. "I can do that."

The Box

Once upon a time there was a little girl. Her parents taught her a lot of messages that parents aren't supposed to teach children: *"No, you don't matter. Your feelings are wrong. You are wrong. Our feelings matter more. You are bad."*

Those messages were too confusing and painful for any little girl to understand. So an angel came down and gave her a box.

"Here," said the angel. "Put those messages in this box."

And so the little girl put the messages in the box. The angel closed the box for her.

Suddenly the little girl didn't hurt so much. She didn't feel very good either. Sort of like . . . emptiness, and disconnected from the world around her. But that was better than the shame of feeling defective and denied love.

As she grew up, she encountered more pain—bullies at school and abusive relationships. Fortunately, she had a solution for those things—the box! She put more bad feelings into the box and felt empty again.

To avoid the feeling of emptiness, she fantasized about finding perfect love from someone else, and she offered perfect love to everyone. She copied other people and acted just like them, so they would *never* want to leave her!

But despite her best efforts, the same thing kept happening . . . over and over again.

And every time, she put the pain in a box and started over, determined to find the person who would make her feel whole and loved.

Except the box was starting to get full. It started to spill over, and she couldn't control it. She cried and yelled at people she cared about, which made them leave. Then she felt ashamed and buried those things deeper in the box, and struggled to keep it shut.

"Why does the same thing keep happening to me?" she

screamed. "Why does the world hate me? All I need is the perfect lover, and then I will be happy. But you keep sending me pain and rejection. I can't take it anymore. My box is overflowing. How can I possibly find the perfect lover with this box inside me? I hate it!"

That night, the angel appeared in her dreams.

"Darling, the world does not hate you. The world loves you. I love you. So much. I am trying to guide you down a different path than the one you're taking. I am trying to burst open your box, so you can feel the pain from so long ago—and heal it. But every time I remind you of this pain, you feel betrayed and block it away. It is not betrayal. It is an opportunity to finally open the box and become the pain inside.

"You can spend the rest of your life running from this intolerable feeling of inner defectiveness that arises when you're abandoned or rejected. You can keep avoiding it with grandiose fantasies and drama and crises and accomplishments and impulsive behaviors, but those things will not help you.

"I gave you the box long ago because you were only a child and had no other way to cope. But you are an adult now, and you do not need this box. You can experience the pain inside, and you can find the true love on the other side—my love—the love you have always sought from others, inside your own heart."

When the girl awoke, she realized—for the first time in her life—just how loved she had *always been*. So she looked down at the box and said:

"Okay, I'm ready."

And the angel watched proudly as the child began her long journey home.

Fear: Anxiety and Depression

'Twas grace that taught my heart to fear,
And grace my fears relieved.

—"AMAZING GRACE"

Continue to decline what your protective self wants—the approval of others, external achievements, material things acquired in a frenzy, and so on. Without these old distractions, you'll be spending more and more time with your version of numbness. Between this and letting go of resentments, your mind will desperately try to get you back to the old way of thinking, panicking that you are getting closer and closer to the wounded place. Because you are.

One of the protective self's most common trigger responses is anxiety. It typically will not present the true wounding to you at first, but instead manifest as vague fear and dread. Although it feels uncomfortable, fear is actually one of the shortcuts back into your body, loud and impossible to contain. It disrupts your comfortable life and forces you to turn your attention inward. It will course through your body as anxiety and depression, tearing apart the protective self that was built up. Old coping mechanisms no longer seem to work, suddenly you're feeling exposed and out of control.

As you get closer to your core wound, expect to feel like the world is closing in on you, expecting the worst at any turn. When we *feel* bad about ourselves, the world seems dangerous

and frightening. Oftentimes we find our worst fears playing over
and over again in our minds.

A lot of times people get to this step, and they think, "What
the hell, why did I do this? I feel so much worse than I did before." But if you are experiencing depression and anxiety, you
are actually making progress. It means you're *finally* in touch
with your body. You are no longer dissociated from your true
feelings, distracted by grandiosity, numbness, and manic energy.
Sleep disturbances and energy deterioration are the body's way
of regulating the protective self's false energy. If your old coping
mechanisms don't make you feel good anymore, you're forced to
seek out other solutions.

We really want to start shifting from a perspective of "Oh
my God, what is happening to me" toward the friendly curiosity of mindfulness. When we do this, we become more comfortable with discomfort, so that it can finally begin expressing itself
to us.

Many people start seeking help because of the depression
and anxiety. Getting help (most commonly in the form of talk
therapy) is a really important step. I think therapy can benefit
anyone, especially if you are suffering from clinical depression,
have suicidal thoughts, or require medication. But keep in mind
that depression and anxiety are not always your enemy. They
are often your body saying, "No more. What we're doing is not
working." You should *expect* things to get worse long before they
get better. If you're lucky, forces will align to trigger old unbearable feelings when you're at your most vulnerable, so you can
finally remember what this feels like and resolve it.

Anxiety is an interesting thing, because it seems to add a layer of fear onto everything. It can take over all of your thoughts. This can lead to intrusive thoughts, where your mind becomes a total jerk and intentionally tries to think of things that upset you. This could be imagining bad or scary things happening to you or the people you love. It could also be having mean or nasty thoughts about people you love. Another common one is thoughts that you're faking your healing, making no progress, or destined to fail "just like all your other attempts."

Don't try to stop or control this voice. Just let it be there, and notice how *mean* it is. It's like an inner bully. This voice *wants* you to believe it is the ultimate truth.

In their book *The Marriage of Spirit*, Leslie Temple-Thurston and Brad Laughlin wrote, "The fear is the warning sign on the gate that says do not go past this point at all costs! Fear is just the veil, which is designed to hold the boundaries of the ego in place so that the pattern does not change or expand."

Anxiety and intrusive thoughts can be really upsetting, but you can take back the reins. This is where mindfulness shines. Instead of trying to stop or control the thoughts, you can watch them non-judgmentally and just let them do their thing. Combine this with unconditional love: the confident and kind energy that just shakes its head and smiles at fear.

As always, be aware of the differences between the protective self's fear and fear that arises from your actual body. For individuals with BPD, the protective self will repeatedly drill its "fears" into you—fears of being abandoned, or being sick, or that others hate you, or dying in a mass casualty event. These are obsessive and dramatic "thinking" fears projected by the protective self. I am looking for you to slow down, and experience the fear felt in your body. These fears slow you down, and you will not feel compelled to tell other people about them for comfort or sympathy. The goal here is not to think yourself into a panic attack, but to calm down and sit with the sensation of fear in your body.

For people with C-PTSD and survivors of cluster-B relationships, don't try to think your way into fear. Let it happen naturally as you experiment with letting down the guard you've built up over the years. What is the guard protecting you from? It's probably not just protecting you from psychopaths and narcissists. It's protecting you from fears about yourself.

Anxiety and depression are serious conditions. If it feels intolerable, you should seek professional help. But I strongly encourage you to stay the path and think of it like a virus working through your system. Remember the unconditional love from our Tools section. It beckons to you, nodding encouragingly and calling for you to carry on. Ask it for help, ask it what it wants from you. I promise, you are finding your way home.

The Core Wound

Eventually we find the core wound: a seemingly unresolvable mess of guilt, shame, worthlessness, and rejection. Layers upon layers of misery. When these feelings begin to leak through again, it'll be like you've been teleported into the past. There will be an innate sense of "I'm bad" that demands you listen to it, over and over again.

Tara Brach uses a phrase that works perfectly here: "Real, but not true."

In order to resolve these feelings, you need to be willing to stay with the wound. That doesn't mean you need to accept it as the truth (because it isn't). But you do need to acknowledge it is a real part of yourself, and approach it, sit with it, even hold it close.

Listen for a perpetually mean voice that doubts and rejects any kindness you're offering it. The part of you that says: *"This love stuff doesn't apply to you, because you're bad and you know it. You're the exception. You're different. You're separate. You're a liar. You're just trying to make yourself feel better, but it's all fake."*

Do not run from this voice or try to change it. Just notice it and calmly stay with it.

You've been brought back to a time in your life when you were completely powerless and helpless. A darkness that nearly destroyed you. Do you see how and why the protective self took over? There is so much self-loathing and self-blame that no human being can function like this. And so in place of genuine self-worth, we developed this protective self that sought worth from the outside, because our inside was so deeply damaged.

When we feel this rejected self, it will seem mangled beyond repair. What are we supposed to do with this? Where is the love we were promised?

PART 4

Resolving the Core Wound

Rejection, betrayal, and abandonment are the emotions
that the ego experiences after what we call the "fall,"
the apparent original disconnect and separation from
Source . . . Somewhere deep in the recesses of our mind is the
memory of a rejection that was more than we could bear,
and continue to run away from.

—LESLIE TEMPLE-THURSTON, *RETURNING TO ONENESS*

The whole reason we deconstructed the protective self was so that we could get to the core wound. Once you get to this point, your entire healing journey is going to change. You'll know when you get here, because you'll feel really bad. You'll probably think, "What the hell, Jackson? Thanks for writing a book that makes me feel like garbage."

But I promise I have a plan.

Remember, the core wound was blocked out because it felt so unbearably bad when it occurred. It's *supposed* to feel bad this time around too. The difference is that this time, you have a lot of new tools and perspectives to do things differently.

Resolving the core wound is going to be a much different path than deconstructing the protective self. That was all about self-awareness and discipline, stopping the distractions and turning your attention inward. Now that those things have happened, the protective self is broken forever. Your mind's old work-around to the core wound is permanently gone.

So our diagram on the opposite page has gotten even simpler. It's just you and the wound now.

Resolving the core wound is all about identifying and exploring different types of suffering. Now that we aren't automatically avoiding our pain, we are able to experience it fully. We are able to remain present in our bodies, even though it doesn't feel very good. The goal is to discover where this core wound came from, what its message is, and eventually release it.

Now that you've un-numbed the wound, you can do the real work.

For many people, these wounds arose in childhood—probably from a parent or trusted caregiver. For others, especially those with C-PTSD that came about later in life, the core wound may have come from a traumatic experience or difficult rejection. For example, people always say cluster-B breakups don't feel like normal breakups. That's because they're *not* normal breakups. In addition to the "normal" emotional loss that comes

EXTERNAL MEASURES OF WORTH REMOVED

Mindfulness/Unconditional Love

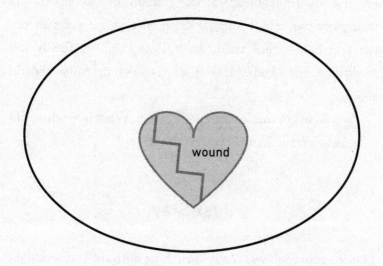

during a breakup, they have also passed along a very persistent wound that lives inside of you—a doubt about yourself.

As long as this wound is numbed out, you cannot make progress. You are running in circles. But now that you've un-numbed the wound, you can do the real work. You're not just spinning your wheels trying to engage with a protective self that could never be healed or improved.

The more time you spend with this wound, the less uncomfortable it will become. After five years of asking therapists and Google, "What is this tight feeling in my heart?," I was no longer asking about the tight feeling. I was asking about things like shame, inadequacy, and resentment. Finally, I was in touch with my body's actual experience. Finally, things were changing. I was honestly happy to feel this bad.

I'm not suggesting we should all feel excited about misery, but it definitely helps to feel grateful for the opportunity to explore our actual internal experience. After years or decades of being stuck inside an infinite loop, we finally feel something real. And *that* is at least something to be hopeful about.

So you've got this wound inside of you. What is it, where did it come from, and how do you resolve it?

Just Stay

The protective self was always searching outwardly for solutions and ideas. Now you've got this rejected self that feels incredibly unbearable. All you need to do is stay with it, just like you would with a wounded animal. Do not try to fix or save it. Just slow down, offer love, and sit with it. Like an ice cube, it will continue to melt and expose new parts of itself.

Last time you were in this place, you didn't know what you were feeling or how to heal it. And so the protective self formed. This time, you are developing the tools to heal so that you can finally resolve this wound. Continue asking the unconditional love for help, over and over again.

This can take many months or years. There is no rush. You're essentially sitting with years or decades of ignored emotions. All you need to do is listen and respond only with kindness. You do not need to judge or analyze what's going on. Instead, simply welcome these feelings. Let them in.

This nurturing process is essential toward building your love, experiencing unfelt emotions, and maturing past the core wound where development stopped.

During this time, you should expect your energy levels to drop significantly. Sleep may be disturbed. Things are going to slow down a lot, and that's a good thing. You are basically rejoining the wavelength of your pain, which you've been dissociated from for quite some time. Old coping methods from the protective self simply won't work anymore. You might slip back into the false energy every now and then, but it won't last long because your old solution is broken.

As you develop the unconditional love, what you're essentially looking for is where your body or mind *resists* this love. One of the most persistent and difficult "resisters" is toxic shame.

The default human response to intolerable shame or rejection is to avoid it. Unfortunately, in our avoidance, we end up behaving in more shame-inducing ways, which just keeps us stuck in our avoidance. Shame triggers impulsivity, addiction, and obsession. By keeping us focused outwardly, it accomplishes the simple task of preventing us from experiencing our shame. But once we realize that shame cannot destroy us (although it certainly feels that way), we can stay with it until we finally stop running.

We finally stop running.

We may not be comfortable or happy yet, but we're no longer living a life of avoidance. We can notice when that nasty self-doubting voice comes out, and we can acknowledge it rather than try to escape from it. This is a truly empowering skill to develop, because it allows us to remain calm despite an inner storm of discomfort.

When we stay with shame, we are learning how to tolerate pain. The more we can do this, the more our bodies will reveal their truth to us. Instead of instinctually avoiding pain, we can meet it with kindness and curiosity. We can ask it questions and learn about it, without being consumed by it.

And then as we explore this uncomfortable truth in our bodies, we can begin to learn and practice the tools needed to release this discomfort, once and for all.

Toxic Shame

> *Toxic shame is the feeling that we are somehow inherently defective, that something is wrong with our being. Guilt is "I made a mistake, I did something wrong." Shame is "I'm a mistake, something is wrong with me." At the core of our wounding is the unbearable emotional pain resulting from having internalized the false message that we are not loved because we are personally defective and shameful.*
>
> —ROBERT BURNEY

Shame itself is not inherently a bad emotion. Shame can be helpful to identify when you've done something wrong and motivate you to reconcile it (and avoid doing it again in the future). The problem is when shame goes from an emotion to an identity. Instead of "you've done something bad," the message becomes "*you* are bad." This is toxic shame, and this is how we end up rejecting our true selves.

This doesn't happen on purpose, it's just a coping mechanism when a trusted loved one rejects or harms us in a very confusing way. Even if we point our fingers and say, "No, *you're* bad!" the damage is already done. The core belief lives inside of us, and no matter how many people tell us we're good, *we* don't believe it.

Oftentimes we have no idea what these new feelings are (especially when they first occur). All we know is that they feel unbearably bad—like a black sludge that suffocates your heart and silences all the things that make life worth living.

Internalized shame messages come from *external* actions or events, especially from those we care about. For example, imagine a little kid whose dad ignores him, breaks promises, and misses his ball games. If this kid came crying to you, what would you say? Chances are, you'd offer comfort and compassion, and assure him it isn't his fault.

With toxic shame, that's not what happens.

Imagine instead that you told the little kid it was *his* fault. Imagine you said, "You're bad and defective, and that's why your dad ignores you. Your feelings are wrong and you are wrong."

The kid then spends a lifetime trying to prove himself and his worth, so his dad will finally acknowledge his existence.

Heartless, right? But that's the bullying voice of toxic shame, and it's a voice so many of us unknowingly carry inside of us.

Again, we have mistakenly taken on these *internal* messages based on *external* events. Some other examples:

- If someone abandoned you after your repeated efforts, you might absorb the message: "I can never do enough. I must prove that I can accomplish and do enough."
- If someone blames you for everything, you might absorb the message: "It's all my fault. I must prove that I am good."
- If someone calls you crazy and abusive, you might absorb the message: "I must be crazy. I am bad and need to hide my true feelings and needs."
- If someone cheats on you and seems much happier without you, you might absorb the message: "I must be inadequate. Other people are better than me."
- If you share your trauma with someone you trust and they dismiss or judge you, you might absorb the message: "I am a liar. My experience isn't true."

Basically, someone else's *external* words and behaviors plant a sense of *inner* defectiveness in you. And who knows, maybe it was *your own* words or behaviors that planted this inner defectiveness—it doesn't matter! Either way, it's an awful feeling, and no one should have to live with that. As evidenced by the protective self, this feeling is often so painful that the body numbs it out and turns the focus externally to keep you distracted.

Once you un-numb it, it can feel relentless. Unconditional

love can help you understand that toxic shame's message is inaccurate, but it may hang on tightly in the body and psyche.

It's really no surprise that many personality disordered individuals are unable to feel remorse for their actions. Their bodies have blocked them from feeling shame, because that emotion nearly destroyed them. But along with shame, they blocked out everything else. In order to feel attachment and love, we *must* find a way to reenter that wounded place. When our core feeling is "bad self," even if we aren't aware of it, we can never successfully love or attach to someone, because we've been shut out from our own true selves.

When we carry toxic shame inside of us, it's like we always have this big secret that we're hoping nobody discovers. We work overtime to hide our secret, masking it with various external enhancements. But no matter how hard we try to hide it, it always seems to follow us. We're constantly afraid that others have figured us out. This has also been described as "imposter syndrome," a feeling that you might be exposed as a fraud at any time. But the only reason you feel like a fraud is because you're hiding an integral part of yourself from others *and* yourself. If you can gather the courage to face this shame, or share it with a professional, you are not hiding anything anymore.

Marriage and family therapist Linda Graham wrote in her article "The Power of Mindful Empathy to Heal Toxic Shame": "Disgust introjected from the other can be seen as the root categorical emotion of the compound emotion of shame. We may manifest this disgust outwardly as the shaming-blaming part is then projected onto others as a defense or manifest it inwardly as we turn on the self. That critical voice inside is now functioning as our own psyche's best effort to protect ourselves from further shame."

And so you can see, the problem with shame is that we have absorbed incorrect conclusions about ourselves, based on the past actions or reactions of a trusted loved one. These conclusions tend to be quite intense and persistent, with a nagging voice that they are the ultimate truth, and anything else we tell ourselves is just a lie to make ourselves feel better.

As long as we carry toxic shame, it is a literal struggle to exist in *our own* bodies. We are constantly thrashing about, like a fish out of water, desperately trying to get away from that unbearable sensation. But no matter how hard we try, how much we distract, how much we run—our bodies are always with us, and so is the shame.

Leslie Temple-Thurston wrote, "When the ego feels it has suffered a loss, the mental, emotional, and physical bodies contract and lose their light. They become deprived of energy, or life force. This loss of life force brings up deep-seated fears in the ego that make it react with certain behaviors, such as the need to defend and protect itself from further loss."

We carry this shame with us in hopes of preventing it from happening again, but that is not the right approach. If someone clocks me in the head with a frying pan, that's going to hurt like hell. In order to remember that it hurts, do I need to hit myself with a frying pan every day? I sure hope not. So let's all put down the frying pan of shame and find a better path forward.

Avoidant and Toxic Shame

"How have you been feeling, with the numbness subsiding?" asked my therapist.

"Still bad!" I said enthusiastically. "Like you said, it's like I'm actually experiencing all of the crap I put my characters through. I wish I wrote nicer books."

She laughed. "What kinds of things are you experiencing?"

"There's just this constant gross feeling of rejection and inadequacy inside of my heart and stomach," I said. "And then that mean, judgy voice that comes up, telling me it's all my fault."

"Maybe your psychologist friend's voice?"

"Probably," I said. "How weird is that, like I've adopted it as my own inner voice."

"Right, we're going to say farewell to that one."

"Even when I'm talking to you right now, I have her relentless voice that says I'm lying to you and I'm bad and I have to admit I'm bad. Like I'm not telling you the whole story, and only telling you things from my side so you'll sympathize with me."

"That's so fantastic that you've noticed this, Jackson. Seriously, it's hard to sit with this stuff without getting consumed by it."

"Thanks," I said. "I wish I could feel good about it all, but this stuff just blocks out feeling good about anything."

"Yes, it does," she said. "That's shame for you. It blocks everything that feels good."

"So what am I supposed to do with this?" I asked. "I don't want to listen to this voice forever."

"I think you already wrote the answer," she said.

"I did?"

"Yes, in your political thriller. Remember? The angry lady learned how to relax and take care of the inadequate guy, and they left the judgmental therapist behind. They're all parts of you."

"Wow, cool!" I said. "I'm sort of doing the first part, but I don't know how to get rid of the judgy, mean voice. Do I need to heal that too?"

"No, I think your book had the right answer," she said. "You have to let go of shame. You have to leave it behind."

Self-Doubt

You should expect a considerable amount of self-doubt through the rest of this journey, a voice telling you "This isn't real" or "My feelings are fake." Include this in your mindfulness, and ask for help from the unconditional love.

Why does this voice exist inside you?

Given that psychological abusers minimize and dismiss your emotions, it's quite common in this process to think "This is stupid" or "I'm making this all up" or "I'm actually to blame." In fact, you might notice a lot of your healing has been done from the mind-set of "What's wrong with me?" Again, just include these in your loving awareness. It won't be easy at first, because these anxieties and doubts have been etched deeply in your thinking. But as you embrace these thoughts every day, the awareness will grow stronger.

As it grows stronger, your body will begin to unravel the old wound, piece by piece. The feelings are likely to be overwhelming and intolerable at first. They may wake you up in the middle of the night, feeling stronger and "more real" than the kind awareness. But the more intense these feelings become, the stronger your own unconditional love will become. Because it recognizes the truth: that no human being, yourself included, deserves to feel this way. And it will keep fighting for you.

At some point, you will realize that the "this isn't true" voice is *actually* what isn't true.

Cluster-B Survivor and Self-Doubt

A lot of cluster-B abuse survivors carry a deep fear that they are the crazy, bad, or evil one. This is the result of a really specific type of gaslighting done by cluster-B disordered individuals.

Here is how it works:

1. A disordered individual provokes you.
2. You deal with the issue calmly, thinking the conflict is resolved.
3. Repeat steps 1 and 2 many, many times.
4. Eventually you react less calmly, sick of the provocations.
5. The disordered individual victimizes themselves from your reaction: "Oh wow, you're so [crazy/sensitive/impatient/mean/bitter]!"

You are then left worrying, "Oh no, am I really [crazy/sensitive/impatient/mean/bitter]?" Before you know it, *you're* apologizing to *them* for a minor *onetime* reaction, even though they were hurting you *repeatedly* in steps 1 and 2 (without ever apologizing). Oftentimes, this triggers people into trying to prove their patience and flexibility by putting up with even *more* of the abuse.

But the issue here wasn't your reaction. It was the repeated abuse that led you to react. They are provoking reactions in you, then invalidating your reactions. This is extremely dangerous for your heart and mind. The disordered individual will rarely (if ever) take responsibility for those things. Instead, they will continue to push you over the edge until you react, so they can prove you're "bad." This false equivalency (my abuse = your reaction) keeps them in control and allows them to continue the abuse.

You might think you'll be the magical exception by *never* reacting to their behavior and remaining calm 100 percent of the time. Nope. Even if you do that, they'll just invent outrageous lies to accuse you of—often their very own qualities.

You may look back on your relationship and think, "If only I had been more easygoing, then things could have stayed peaceful." This is an extremely damaging inner belief that will likely lead to your attracting more toxic and selfish energy drainers, and blaming yourself for it.

The protective self is never satisfied (like trying to fill a black hole), the protective self blames you for not filling the void, and so it is always searching outwardly for more. Even if you do everything "right," it will still never be enough. Because no matter what you do, the disordered person still has their inner agitation (which you have no control over). And they blame their inner discomfort on external factors, because that's how the disorder works.

These behaviors, on behalf of the disordered person you were in a relationship with, are indicative of serious psychological damage, and they can only be resolved through long-term intensive self work. You cannot reason with or help another person out of this mind-set. Please do not allow them to erode your self-worth with these games, worsening your inner belief of "never enough." They want you to doubt yourself, because people who doubt themselves are the only people who would ever stick around for their behavior.

Gaslighting implants a constant self-doubting voice inside survivors, causing them to question their every move, interaction, and thought. This is an extremely exhausting way to exist and will eventually lead to anxiety and depression. It also makes them vulnerable to more gaslighting, because their defenses have weakened, and the best gaslighting victims are those who doubt themselves.

As you move forward, please be mindful of this self-doubt. It's normal after cluster-B relationships, but it's not true. Abusers gaslight with such confidence and conviction that it can actually become your own inner voice. It will greatly hinder any progress you make, because you will second-guess your own emotions and instincts. This leads to needing constant external validation, repeating your story to anyone who will listen, but it's still not enough. Deep down *you* don't believe yourself.

You begin to overanalyze and ruminate on every little detail.

You flip-flop back and forth between "my fault" and "their fault." Even when you settle on "their fault," there remains a relentless voice inside of you that questions this.

Mindfulness can help you become aware of this self-doubting inner voice and eventually realize that it is not your own voice. It is the voice of an abuser. And with enough time and self-care, you can release this voice and restore the trust between your mind and emotions.

Self-Forgiveness

Shame comes from a core feeling of "bad self." Self-forgiveness dissolves shame, because when all is forgiven, there is nothing left to be ashamed about. This means forgiving everything, even our deepest dark beliefs about ourselves. Whether these beliefs are true or not is no longer important. With shame-thinking, everything is about self-analysis and judgment—you can only be worthy of love if you are good and correct. With self-forgiveness, the story is no longer important. It's not about being right or wrong. You could be 100 percent wrong and the worst person in the world. If you choose to explore self-forgiveness, you are letting all of those things go.

One of the worst forms of suffering is doing things against our own values. This can cause an intense self-aversion that is not easily remedied. This often leads to shame and distrust in ourselves. From here, the default reaction is to judge and blame the self, along with judging and blaming others. This rigid solution offers some amount of control and helps us feel separate from the "bad self" who violated our values.

With the shame safely locked away behind some logic of "I did X because of Y," we can become the "good self" and ensure we never do those things again. Everything slowly becomes controlled, familiar, and protected. The problem with living like this is that there's zero room for error or vulnerability.

Self-forgiveness is a powerful, light energy force that can dissolve these old walls and bring us back to wholeness. This is not a onetime "breakthrough," but instead a practice that we repeat over and over again until it's our constant state of living. When we offer ourselves forgiveness, we are offering ourselves mercy—which is at the core of unconditional love.

A lot of people think, "This just seems like an easy way to let myself off the hook," or "If I don't accept the blame, I'm not learning any lessons." That's not what self-forgiveness is about at all. Your lessons, wisdom, and knowledge aren't going anywhere. It's not like you're issuing yourself a get-out-of-jail-free card to go behave badly and say, "Doesn't matter, I'm forgiven!" It's simply about dissolving the walls around our hearts so that we can love freely again.

It may feel awkward and hollow at first, because it's just your mind playing ping-pong with yourself. Like, "I forgive myself. . . . Okay, great. Now what?" This is totally normal for an abuse survivor. We become so accustomed to living in the analytical fight-or-flight brain, that the soft feelings aren't there yet. Don't worry, they're still there, and self-forgiveness is the key to unlocking them.

Practice this whenever it feels right. Don't try to force your-self into anything. Just approach it with the gentle care you might offer to a child. For a long time, your analytical brain will be in charge of the show, trying to make connections and problem-solve—seeking breakthroughs and "ah-hah" moments. That's completely fine. The more the mind focuses on self-forgiveness, the more the body will start to catch up.

As the body catches up (which may take many months of practice), waves of raw emotion and feeling will start to come up. Tremendous amounts of guilt, inadequacy, jealousy, and shame. The old analytical mind will snatch back control, be-cause it is terrified of these feelings, of vulnerability. As you watch your mind try to take back control, your feelings will only grow stronger. You will see a self clinging to the story, desper-ately trying to defend its existence and maintain control from the bad thing ever happening again.

The more we watch this self, the more natural self-forgiveness becomes. We see how much we are suffering from these walls, and we start to sense there is something so much better on the other side. When we experience this old shame, we can approach it much differently this time.

Instead of a story, a reason, or an answer, we're letting it *all* go. We are forgiving the "bad self"—the feeling self—so it can be embraced fully, instead of locked away. We stop holding ourselves hostage and stop living a life of pain avoidance. We are accepting the truth that we are human. If we could have done better at the time, we would have. No one willingly seeks unhappiness.

Remember, this is not a logical process, but an emotional and spiritual one. The unconditional love does not love you because of what you did or didn't do. It does not need you to rationalize or explain anything. It needs you to understand, right now in this moment, that everything is forgiven. This was a big "ah-hah" moment for me, because I spent all this time worrying: "What if it really was all my fault? Then I can't forgive myself!" But the whole point of self-forgiveness is realizing even if those darkest fears were true, you are still forgiven and loved. You don't need to prove yourself anymore. That is the power of unconditional love.

A lot of times we don't forgive ourselves because we're afraid we'll do the same bad behavior again, but this is a false sense of control. Shaming ourselves only causes more shameful behavior. It is an infinite loop. We're holding ourselves hostage, which feels terrible, which causes us to act out and make more bad decisions, which causes us to hold ourselves hostage even more intensely. Forgiveness ends this cycle, unlocks your heart, and allows you to start behaving in ways that you're actually proud of. This gets you into a new loop—a virtuous cycle instead of a downward spiral.

You're a human being worthy of love and mercy.

If you can't forgive, can you forgive yourself for being unable to forgive? I know it's a weird question, but that's what unconditional love looks like. It's not about doing it "right" or "perfectly." It's not about holding yourself hostage until you "figure it out." It's okay that you can't do it.

You're a human being worthy of love and mercy. So you're learning how to adopt a newer, more easygoing relationship with yourself.

Something really important to understand about the protective self is that *you didn't ask for it*. Repeat that in your mind a few times: *You didn't ask for the protective self to take over.* This was a physiological response from your own body, tensing or blocking or numbing to protect you. You didn't go through a trauma and say, "Okay, body, numb me out now!" Decisions were made without your approval or awareness. All of us carry different bodily responses to different levels of fear-based situations. It's in our genetic code. Yours was activated for whatever reason, and now you're working on breaking free from it.

I spent hours with therapists, doctors, hypnotists—desperately trying to understand what that "tight feeling" in my heart was. Despite my relentless efforts to get in touch with the sensation, I was not able to. Despite the efforts of supportive and compassionate professionals, I was not able to. In the end, it was actually another relationship that finally reactivated those old feelings.

Carl Jung wrote: "The foundation of all mental illness is the unwillingness to experience legitimate suffering."

I agree with this quote, with one small caveat. The word "unwilling" implies that there is some sort of conscious choice to avoid the suffering. When it comes to these issues, this is not really the case. You may have all the willpower in the world, determined to experience your suffering, but your mind and body have made the decision to keep you out. You must forgive yourself for this, so that you can finally stop being at war with your body.

Cluster-B Survivor and Self-Forgiveness

Mel was making a lot of progress in her recovery. She rarely thought about her ex anymore, but she was stuck with a new problem: she felt deeply ashamed and humiliated about her own behavior in the aftermath of her relationship.

"I just acted so crazy," she said. "It makes me cringe to think back to it."

"But it was just an anomaly," I said. "You reacted normally to an extremely abnormal situation. So many survivors of these relationships behave in uncharacteristic ways after the betrayal."

"I'm usually such a calm and cheerful person," she said. "I acted like a vengeful witch. I was the 'crazy ex' everyone jokes about on sitcoms. Every time I see those jokes I recoil, because I'm like, 'Oh my God, that was me' even though I never wanted to be that way."

"But you're holding yourself hostage over something that happened a long time ago," I said. "Why do you think you can't forgive yourself for that?"

"Because I'm afraid I'll do it again!" she said. "At least this way, I can be sure I never act crazy again. I'm always in control."

"Doesn't that prevent you from loving others completely, and expressing yourself fully?"

"Yes," she said. "I feel like everything is so controlled and careful. But I don't know any other way."

"Self-forgiveness is the other way," I said. "You did things against your values because you were in an impossible situation."

"But what if I wasn't!" she said. "What if I'm actually that nasty crazy person, and the relationship just brought it out in me? What if he wasn't even a psychopath and I'm just a lunatic who made that up to avoid feeling rejected? What if I have borderline personality disorder, and just invented the abuse thing?"

"Let's go with that then," I said. "Let's go with the very worst-case scenario that you are the disordered one and he was a standup guy—who cheated on you and replaced you with another woman while you were still together—but we'll put that aside for now."

She laughed. "Okay, yes, what happens in that scenario?"

"So in that situation, why aren't you worthy of forgiveness? You were some crazy lady. Now you are working hard not to be a crazy lady. Why don't you deserve mercy?"

She looked down. "I don't know."

"Do you deserve to be punished for your past, for the rest of your life?"

"No, I don't think so."

"Me neither. And that's just the worst-case scenario!" I said. "Imagine if he had been some jerk who cheated on you and replaced you with another woman while you were still together . . ."

"Yeah, imagine that." She laughed again.

"So can you see, this really isn't about right or wrong? It isn't about crazy or not crazy. Unconditional love is *un*conditional."

"What about my friends?" she asked. "I acted so crazy in front of them too. One of them doesn't even talk to me anymore, and I just feel this intense dread and shame every time I see her. I'm so embarrassed by my behavior. I have to make sure I never act like that again."

"The thing about withholding forgiveness from yourself is that it makes you behave in more shame-inducing ways. Everything feels sad and heavy and dramatic. When you let it all go, your heart gets light and tingly. Things become funny and easygoing again. Friends will naturally enjoy your company."

"So I won't just go . . . crazy . . . if I forgive myself?"

"No, I am certain that you will not. Your brain and life lessons won't go anywhere. You'll just feel good again. Don't you deserve that?"

She nodded. "I think I do."

Forgiveness

Forgiveness creates the space for love to rush in. For this purpose we can transform the gatekeeper of our heart into a celestial bodyguard, free of all preconceived notions, becoming our heart's greatest ally. Actual forgiveness does not mean allowing someone who wronged you to forego his or her karmic debt, nor does it mean condoning or forgetting what was done.

—GIUDITTA TORNETTA,
CONVERSATIONS WITH THE WOMB

An important note before I begin this section: Predators, abusers, and cults love to use "forgiveness" as a tool to guilt-trip you into giving them another chance. To manipulate you into taking the blame for their own wrongdoings. To prove that you're both "equally as bad." To shame you for legitimate anger you may carry over mistreatment. To wag their fingers at you and patronize you for not being able to "let go" of the past (as opposed to them taking responsibility for their inappropriate behavior).

This type of sanctimonious forgiveness is manipulative and predatory. Do not give second chances to people who express no remorse for their mistreatment of you. Do not give second chances to people who express remorse but continue the same harmful behavior. Do not accept another person forgiving you for crimes you did not commit. The forgiveness I explore in this chapter is intended to protect you from this dangerous gaslighting, while also freeing your heart to new experiences.

Resentment (or non-forgiveness) is natural when we have been unfairly wronged, betrayed, or hurt—especially by someone we trusted. Over time, this causes many symptoms: paranoia, black-and-white thinking, victim mentality, self-pity, unworthiness, lack of self-love, fear of rejection, afraid of loving too much, waiting for a knight in shining armor, blame (of others and self), inability to stop analyzing the past, avoidance and isolation.

Needless to say, it's not fun, and it also feels like further unfairness piled on top of the already unfair situation. Why should you have to deal with these bad feelings because of someone else's bad behavior? Why should you be responsible for letting go or forgiving, when they are the ones who hurt you? This mind-set ironically causes more resentment and victimization. The protective self *loves* to reinforce itself.

Sometimes we think: "Well, that jerk takes their shame out on others. At least I just take it out on myself. I absorb it, and that makes me a better person." While I agree it's good not to harm others, you still *are* harming someone! You are betraying yourself with every unkind, shameful, or bullying thought against yourself. You should feel just as motivated to resolve this as you would be if you were harming other people.

Another common thought pattern is: *"Other people may be able to forgive, but my situation is so much worse and no one has been through it. They wouldn't understand."* Here's another: *"It's not fair that I have to forgive. I'm the one who's hurting and they don't even care."* And finally: *"I hate feeling bitter over something I couldn't control. Now I'm even bitter about feeling bitter!"* These feelings of resentment and injustice are exactly what we want to get in touch with. I called it my *grumbly voice*—it's not just frustration about the original wrongdoing, it's an entire mind-set that *everything* has become unfair. This is the victim identity, which often forms after betrayal. Mindfulness helps you become aware of the thinking without judging it.

I remember some high school classmates used to call me names, making fun of my hair or looks or intelligence. Back then I just joked back or ignored them. Barely gave a second thought to it. I was too busy thinking about cats. But with a more recent traumatic event, and with a new wound in place, I suddenly felt very upset and persecuted by those wrongdoings from a *decade* ago.

This is the nature of emotional wounding—it changes our entire perspective, the lens through which we view the world and ourselves. How could I, the same person as previous me, be offended by things that previous me was *not* offended by? How could I feel victimized by things that once did not feel victimizing?

I also became convinced that there were more loud sounds, sirens, and diesel truck noises than there used to be. God, they were so annoying! Why couldn't they just shut up?

This helped me realize that the common denominator was myself, not the world. It's not that people were always kind and loving in the past, and now people are mean. It's not that the ambulances got louder and more obnoxious. That wasn't why my heart became tight. That would be a very weird wound. No, the world did not become nastier. The main difference was that in the past, hurtful behavior from others did not stick to me like a black sludge.

So how do we lift the black sludge?

Beyond Victimhood

A lot of this journey is about releasing the idea of betrayal from our own hearts so that we can be free. Betrayal convinces us that we are being let down and that it isn't fair (usually after something *actually* unfair happened). Breaking beyond this belief—however true it might have been—allows us to be free and live in the present moment again. This isn't about rewriting history, but rather finding joy and meaning in the process of opening our own hearts.

In *The Way of the Human*, Stephen Wolinsky describes betrayal as a key trigger for core wounding: "One of the major causes for the creation of False Self identities is betrayal. It is a form of chaos which is caused when someone we trust is unfaithful, disloyal, or deceives us in some way. Identities are formed in an attempt to handle or overcome this crisis. Because of this, the nervous system scans the environment to read for possible betrayal, or avoids and defends against possible betrayal as part of the survival mechanism. The problem is that the scanning-searching device is not in present time—but remains in the past time shock and defense against the shock."

In order to overcome the wounding caused by betrayal, we must explore the false messages we absorbed about *ourselves* as a result of the betrayal. Wolinsky writes that this betrayal to ourselves is the only real betrayal, and we must learn how to let it go.

Once again, you should not need to feel compelled to *do* anything as you work on forgiveness. This is an internal process, not one involving reconciliation or contact. Forgiveness is not asking you to pretend it wasn't that bad. It is acknowledging the pain, and accepting that it was real, so that you can learn from it and let it go.

It's really not so much about forgiving or loving the perpetrator as it is about letting go of the victim mind-set that comes from betrayal. If someone dominates or harms us, we are then forced into the role of the "dominated" or "harmed" one: the victim. Essentially, a life event has taught us that bad things are happening to us, we have internalized this story, and our bodies react in kind. We feel sunken, helpless, angry.

But we can release the story the same way it formed. To forgive, you're going to need to adopt a new story. This one lets go of the "perpetrator" and "victim" roles.

To start this perspective shift, it helps to understand that you were almost definitely harmed by someone else's protective self—someone disconnected from unconditional love and therefore extremely misguided. Healer and teacher Robert Burney writes: "There is no blame here, there are no bad guys, only wounded souls and broken hearts and scrambled minds."

I'm not a huge fan of digging into someone else's past or childhood and trying to understand "why" they mistreated me. This gets me sucked into old patterns of feeling sorry and sympathetic, which only invites more misbehavior. You don't need to dive into the perpetrator's suffering or try to invent stories of their suffering. Some people have perfectly fine lives and still treat others like garbage. The point is, this isn't really about them, it's about releasing the messages they left behind in you.

The best way I've seen forgiveness described is from the book *Returning to Oneness*, by Leslie Temple-Thurston:

> It takes more than a one-time forgiveness and is more like learning to live in a continuous state of forgiveness. . . . Having an experience of betrayal means that we are identified with the egoic personality programs that are telling us that we are being let down, taking a loss, experiencing a breach of trust or feeling victimized by something. . . . The scar tissue in the emotional body is the grievance— the holding on to the idea that something bad was done to us. . . . forgiveness actually dissolves the hard knot and releases the contraction, so the energy can get through to your heart. . . . Forgiveness releases the idea of betrayal held in the mind, and the contraction betrayal creates in the physical body leaves. It also releases the associated emotional content.

I highly recommend reading that book's entire chapter on forgiveness (and the whole book too). It helps you see the betrayal from an impersonal perspective, even though betrayals feel very personal. It is not about feeling sympathy or love for the perpetrator, as many classic resources on forgiveness might suggest. Although those things may help you shift your perspective, they are still focused on the other person, who is no longer the real cause of your suffering. That person is likely not even in your life anymore. The cause of the suffering is the *internal* story absorbed from that person, and the mind-set this has caused. This is really about changing that mind-set and letting go of the story.

When others hurt you, this is a reflection of their own demons. They didn't hurt you because there was something defective about you. They hurt you because of their own sense of inner defectiveness that someone likely passed along to them long before they had any idea what to do with it.

This should also help you understand the severity of their damage, so you can protect yourself. Your love or understanding of this person will not prevent them from continuing to harm you, unless they are also doing the hard work to heal themselves. Wounded people may pretend to be healed so that you'll let them back into your life, only to continue to harm you.

So you see, forgiveness and protection actually go together like two good friends. You *need* to learn how to protect yourself, so the protective self doesn't have to.

This allows us to shift from victim mind-set (*"bad* things are happening *to me"*), toward the idea that wounds are being passed along and we no longer choose to carry that wound ("things are happening").

By letting go of the story of betrayal, we are leaving behind an old world. We are no longer defined by the traumatic event, but instead by the love that has freed us from it. Forgiveness becomes much easier (and almost automatic) as we begin to learn that our old shame-based beliefs aren't true. We see someone else acting out their own demons, and recognize it had nothing to do with us.

When we're living in betrayal mind-set, it's like everything gets piled onto the original wound. Every time something goes wrong, the wounding says: "Wow, can you believe this happened, on top of everything else I've been through? The universe must be conspiring against me. I will just keep waiting for something good to happen to cancel it all out." When we let go of the original wound, the new things don't have anything to stick onto anymore. It's like our plumbing has been cleaned out, so stuff can start flowing through again.

We stop seeing our suffering as a personal attack—a persecution. It becomes more about forgiving life (the world, the universe, God) than forgiving any perpetrator. This is how we let go of the betrayal mind-set. Instead, we begin to see our suffering from a less personal, bigger-picture perspective.

As a result, the feeling of forgiveness is light and joyful, almost humorous, as the tension in the chest dissolves. As you let go of the story in your mind, the body follows. It took me many months of meditating on forgiveness to experience this sensation, but eventually your body will feel it—it's a mind-set, one that you can experiment with during meditation and eventually decide to adopt permanently. It disconnects you from the old story, and all of the painful sensations that came with it.

More than any other healing technique, forgiveness brought bliss to my heart and mind. I could physically feel it. At first, I could only experience it during meditation with music. But with time, I found I could "switch it on" anytime, sitting at my desk or at the gym. Eventually, we can make the final choice to stay there as the default mode.

Things that you once obsessed or ruminated about no longer have anything to land on. You have new lessons to protect yourself, while also letting go of the victim identity that forms after betrayal.

Many times, people approach forgiveness in a way that only invites more suffering into their lives. This was my approach for a while. Of course, this only led to more of the same pain, and therefore a very negative understanding of forgiveness.

Codependency and Forgiveness

If you're a codependent, odds are you've been doing forgiveness wrong your entire life. This misguided version of forgiveness can destroy your life and even have you apologizing to people who harmed *you*.

When codependents first explore forgiveness, they may see it as a sign that they need to allow everyone into their lives and become even *more* trusting. They may think they need to just forget everything they've learned and drop all boundaries. Early attempts at forgiveness actually illuminate the deepest roots of codependent thinking—believing it's all about "being selfless," absorbing blame, and focusing on other people.

Codependents will usually "forgive" everything, even the most awful behavior. Over and over again. Until one day the betrayal is so terrible that they finally snap. Suddenly their forgiveness is replaced by overwhelming resentment.

Now the idea of forgiveness is unacceptable. Absolutely not! This person overstepped their boundaries too many times. Forgiving would make you a pushover. It would mean going back to that terrible behavior—giving them another chance.

But forgiveness is actually the opposite. It's not pretending things "weren't that bad" or inventing sympathetic qualities in a perpetrator. It is recognizing and accepting the full extent of the damage this person caused, and choosing not to carry it as your own damage anymore. It means you can walk away much faster the next time.

It does not have to include reconciliation or contact of any kind. It is an internal process. If at any point your forgiveness process convinces you to invite an abuser back into your life (or even talk to them), this is not the kind of forgiveness we're looking for. It will actually impede your own progress.

Codependent forgiveness is this fantasized tear-filled beautiful reconciliation where everything is magically cured by love and compassion. As with most codependent issues, it's focused on other people. *Their* problems. *Their* childhood. *Their* past. You think you understand them so much, maybe even more than they understand themselves! You make up excuses and reasons for them, your heart melts, you take them back, and then they hurt you again.

No wonder a codependent's protective self holds on to resentment! It's terrified that if you forgive, you'll go running right back to that person. You practically *need* resentment for survival. But when you truly love and care for yourself, you do not need resentment to leave a toxic situation. Self-love is a far greater (and more pleasant) motivator.

BPD and Forgiveness

BPD is a maladaptive coping mechanism based on nonforgiveness and victimhood (which at some point you probably *needed* to survive). If you release those things, you release the control that BPD has over you. And it will put up one hell of a fight to maintain that control.

When the protective self is in charge, BPD is all about "bad things are happening to me." That's the entire modus operandi. Feeling victimized, betrayed, abused, and abandoned by others. While this may have been true at some point, the protective self sees it even when it is not happening. The BPD protective self identifies as the suffering "pain" identity. It views itself as the tragic victim who is always being hurt. It fantasizes about being the "damsel in distress" who is saved by a knight in shining armor. It even fantasizes about being harmed or tortured so that others will feel sorry for it and rescue it.

But this victim identity is *not who you are*. And the protective self likely feels angry or defensive at this suggestion! Because victimhood is all it knows. It relies on victimhood to extract sympathy and love from others. Without the victim identity, it has no idea who or what it is.

People with BPD often struggle with identity issues, wondering who they truly are and what they think. Victimhood is not the true self. It is an addictive and tempting role to take on, but it is not your identity.

> Victimhood is not the true self. It is an addictive and tempting role to take on, but it is not your identity.

It also blocks healing, because it keeps you stuck on a hamster wheel searching for more traumas and betrayals to explain your unhappiness. It's extremely common for people with BPD to think: "I must have been sexually abused as a child, that's why I'm so messed up!" While it's extremely important to explore that in therapy if it happened to you, most people with BPD are trying to explain their inner discomfort with external stories and reasons.

This doesn't make you a bad person. Remember, you did not ask the protective self to take over. But now that you're aware of it, you can see its tricks and stop searching for trauma after trauma to explain your empty feeling. Otherwise, you will begin to see others as dominators or perpetrators or abusers, even when they are treating you well.

This causes a much bigger issue, where you lose the ability to trust yourself and know when your intuition is detecting legitimate danger, as opposed to *splitting* on someone who cares about you.

The previous paragraph tends to trigger intense feelings of dread and discomfort in borderline individuals, because it brings them closer to the shame of "What if it's all my fault and I ruin all of the good things in my life?" It is extremely important to explore this sensation, rather than try to distract yourself from it. *That* is the exact sensation we want to get in touch with during all of this work.

Once you release the constant underlying shame, you are left only with the truth. You can easily identify situations where your behavior may have driven people away, without that meaning you're somehow a bad person. Instead of needing a victim story to mask your shame, you are facing your shame head-on so that it can be released (which coincidentally tends to stop the behavior that drives people away to begin with).

Forgiveness helps you to restore your intuition, because you are not carrying past betrayals and applying them to others. You are seeing each person as their own individual experience, and therefore able to recognize when something seems off. You are also not carrying around your *own* past betrayals, which lowers your self-worth and keeps you stuck in bad situations.

You may feel unable to forgive yourself because you don't think you "deserve" forgiveness. Again, this is your shame talking. It convinces you that if you forgive yourself, then you're letting yourself off the hook and you'll just keep doing bad things. You think if you lash yourself repeatedly, then at least you'll stay in control. But self-forgiveness isn't a free pass to behave badly. It's about understanding the impact your actions have on others, taking responsibility to prevent it from happening again, and choosing not to carry self-hatred about the past anymore (with the understanding that self-hatred only causes you to do more shameful and impulsive things). If you really want to help the people in your life, the best thing you can do is learn to *forgive yourself*—not lash yourself over and over again. This doesn't help anyone.

People with BPD should also be particularly careful about not using forgiveness to feed the protective self. It tends to get manically excited about healing ideas and then get bored when there's no immediate gratification. You may find that you get the sudden urge to tell an old ex you forgive them for abusing you, or reach out to a past friend for abandoning you. But if they don't reply in the way you expect (or at all), you feel angry and betrayed. You may be forgiving them for things they didn't actually do, unintentionally solidifying the protective self's victim story.

This becomes especially apparent if a person with BPD discovers that an ex or loved one is seeking support for the way they were treated. This can cause a person with BPD to react with extreme rage and panic. Even though the stories of harmful behavior are often true, they feel angry at the idea of someone else being their "victim."

Forgiveness is about taking personal responsibility and acknowledging the wounds we pass along to others, as well as those passed along to us. Then we can stop trying to control the narrative, have the last word, or be the bigger victim. If we harm someone else, they have every right to seek support.

Once again, none of these situations are about actual forgiveness—they are all about the protective self trying to control things, or achieve a desired outcome. If you find yourself going down this path, spend more time with the empty feeling before approaching forgiveness. You should not feel compelled to contact anyone or "correct the record."

Cluster-B Abuse Survivor and Forgiveness

When you live with resentment, you close your hands tightly around your heart, hoping that no one will penetrate this strong-fisted protection. When you forgive, you open those hands, let your heart out to love again, freely and confidently. Why? Because evil cannot defeat you; evil cannot destroy your heart's capacity to love.

—DR. ROBERT ENRIGHT

Forgiveness after cluster-B abuse can seem impossible, and the mere suggestion can be extremely upsetting to someone who has experienced such remorseless abuse. The word "forgiveness" alone tends to bring about angry reactions in the cluster-B recovery community. And for good reason. This person likely played on your compassion and forgiveness over and over again. Every time you tried to protect yourself, they knew exactly what to say to lure you back in and make you feel sorry for them. Untreated personality disordered individuals are masters at pity stories and making themselves seem like the sympathetic victim, even when they're the ones causing harm. They often present a childlike innocence to the world, while they are abusing and manipulating you behind closed doors.

So how in the world are you supposed to forgive someone like that, someone who sees forgiveness as a weakness to be exploited?

The first step, which may not sound like forgiveness at all, is to stop allowing them into your life. As long as this person is guided by their protective self, you are pouring your energy and love into a black hole. Their protective self is kept alive by attention, control, and sympathy. Unless this person goes through *years* (not weeks or months) of intensive therapy, there is absolutely no chance that they have changed. They may be able to hide their symptoms for a few months, making promises of change to get your hopes back up, but their hurtful behavior will always come creeping back.

People with cluster-B disorders will often say exactly the right thing to get you back under their control. They'll admit their faults, sob and grovel, call themselves a monster, even commit to therapy. But it won't be lasting change, because it wasn't real to begin with. Forgiveness starts with understanding the true severity of these disorders. The disorder is so ingrained in the fabric of their personality that any promise of change must be disregarded as part of their disorder.

People cannot go from abusing and manipulating you one day, to magically being healed a week later. This is simply impossible. Especially when this change occurs as a response to possible abandonment or rejection, there's just no chance this is authentic change. The person may *wish* it was authentic in the moment, they may even convince themselves it's authentic, but it is not authentic because it is coming from the protective self.

The more we come to understand our own protective self, the easier it becomes to see the extent of the damage needed to cause the cluster-B disorders. In *Psychopath Free*, I stated that psychopaths don't feel insecurity or shame. This is true in a way, although my perspective has shifted. They don't feel those things, because, I believe, those things have been numbed from their consciousness.

Despite all their confidence and charisma, anyone with a cluster-B disorder will describe a constant nagging boredom or emptiness that follows them wherever they go. As long as they carry that sensation, they cannot provide you with authentic change. They can provide you with promises, convincing "ah-hah" moments, and dramatic reconciliations. But not change.

As you're discovering through this book, getting in touch with numbing sensations like "emptiness" or "boredom" takes a lot of time, therapy, patience, and adversity. It requires slowing down in life, quelling grandiose thinking, dropping the blame game, and exploring extremely painful feelings of shame. No one can accomplish that in a month or two.

Why am I putting all of this in the Forgiveness section? Because I'm trying to illustrate how well forgiveness and protection go together. Once you understand the underlying damage of a cluster-B disorder, you will stop trying to make contact. You will stop trying to save or fix the person. You will stop trying to restore your "perfect" relationship.

Then we get to the best part of forgiveness. If you were harmed by someone else's protective self, the resulting wound is meaningless. This may sound cavalier, but I'm serious. So often we see our abusers as these dominating figures who trigger deep feelings of rejection, shame, and inadequacy. We scurry around trying to prove we're happy, fantasizing about rejecting them the way they rejected us, obsessively analyzing and diagnosing them to regain some sense of control.

But when we look at things from the bigger picture, staying with our pain and keeping forgiveness in mind, the old wound dissolves. The roles of victim and victimizer don't mean anything. It was all an illusion, a projection from their protective self—and therefore our victimhood was created from an illusion. It was nothing more than a wound passed along to us. Instead of keeping this wound as our own (or passing it along to others), it begins to dissolve from our identity, once and for all.

Boundaries

Some people, when they first get into Recovery, when they first start on a healing path, mistakenly believe that they are supposed to take down their defenses and learn to trust everyone. That is a very dysfunctional belief. It is necessary to take down the dysfunctional defense systems but we have to replace them with defenses that work. We have to have a defense system, we have to be able to protect ourselves. There is still a hostile environment out there full of wounded Adult Children whom it is not safe to trust.

—ROBERT BURNEY, *CODEPENDENCY:*
THE DANCE OF WOUNDED SOULS

During the entire year that I wrote this book, this section remained blank until the very end. I just kept scrolling past the big "Boundaries" title, and then going to work on a different chapter instead. I knew it was an important topic, but I also felt completely unqualified to talk about it—because for the majority of my life, I've had really bad boundaries.

Normally when kids touch a hot stove, they learn to never touch the hot stove again. In this metaphor, I'm a different type of kid who touches the hot stove again. And again. And again. And then I decide to put my face on the hot stove. And then I sit down on the hot stove and sauté myself in some garlic butter.

I used to ask friends and family for advice about various situations. "Is this acceptable or weird?" Ninety-nine percent of the time, if I had to ask, I already knew the answer. And then they told me the answer too: "It's weird." Then I proceeded to ignore my intuition *and* their intuition. Then something weird happened.

So when it comes to the subject of boundaries, I really felt like the blind leading the blind.

I don't have any sort of attraction to pain or suffering. I go to great lengths to avoid those things, and I have a vetting process that I like to think is pretty comprehensive. The problem was that I failed to act when people showed me their true colors. I did not focus on actions, but instead on words and fantasies.

Someone could literally say to me, "Jackson, I'm a horrible person. I'm mean and manipulative," and I would say to them, "Aww, no, you're not! You're a good person." Then they'd do something mean or manipulative, and I'd think to myself, "What the hell, that's so unfair, I was always so nice to you!"

Hopefully you can see that this is Very Stupid.

It's fine to see the good in people, but when someone tells you who they are, it's a good idea to listen. When someone *shows* you who they are, then you really should be paying attention.

For a long time, I hung on to this idea that psychopaths and narcissists acted as perfect mirror images in the beginning, and there was absolutely nothing I could have ever done to prevent what happened. How could poor innocent me have ever detected that my "soul mate" had another side to him? The idealization was too perfect, too seamless, undetectable!

But when I look back now, I realize that's just not true. There were many moments of unkindness, criticism, and attention seeking—some of which occurred quite early on. But instead of trusting myself, I overlooked these issues and tried to keep the peace.

There was just something in me that automatically doubted myself, wondered if I was being unreasonable, and decided to be "nice" and forget about it. Then I felt shocked and betrayed when he ended up being a jerk. But really, what did I expect? I was so distracted with my own fantasies and hopes that I ignored reality.

I don't mean any of this as victim blaming. The fault of abuse goes on the abuser. But unfortunately we don't live in a utopian world where everyone is nice, so we must also learn how to love and protect *ourselves*.

Because I repeatedly skipped that step, my body took over and started playing guardian for me. The problem is, the body's guard can be very difficult to communicate with when you have no idea what's going on inside of your body. Especially in the case of trauma, when your body decides to permanently activate the guard, thereby making everyone look like a threat. What good is an alarm that's ringing 24/7?

When we start learning mindfulness, we are finally learning how to communicate with our bodies. If we listen to its messages, we learn a lot of things. We find things that need to be released (like shame and guilt and self-doubt), but we also find some things that need more attention. If your body is trying to protect you, that means there's something worth protecting. It wants the best for you. It wants for you to be happy and have your needs met. If you're not making this happen, it will find some unpleasant ways to nudge you in the right direction.

The great thing about mindfulness and unconditional love is that we start to spend a lot of time getting in touch with difficult sensations. It's sort of like going on a long and challenging adventure with ourselves. As we spend all this time with ourselves, we learn to like this person inside of our bodies. This person who struggles, succeeds, fails, and tries their best. We start to care about this person.

This is not the same sort of self-love that comes from narcissism. It's not about declaring to the world how sexy or successful or smart we are. It's a much quieter, more authentic care that we express toward ourselves. Like a friend or child that we're proud to know.

And would you put that friend or child in harm's way? Would you toss them blindly into the arms of a love-bombing date? Would you tell them to give a fourth chance to an abusive partner? Would you tell them to remain in a friendship with a critical, judgmental control freak? Would you tell them they deserve their shame because they're a wretched person?

I hope not!

Boundaries seem to be a natural by-product of actually liking ourselves. When we care about this person inside of us, we want what's best for that person. So it starts to become much easier to stand up for yourself, say no, or discuss your needs.

When the body is in charge of protection, things are pretty volatile and unpleasant. You'll be okay with unacceptable treatment for a long time, until one day your body says, *"No more!"* and then you lash out and people wonder what the heck is wrong with you. After all, you accepted their treatment up until this point with a polite smile on your face.

When you take the reins into your own hands, you are saying: "It's okay, body. You can relax. I've got this now." But you have to actually *got this*. You can't just say that, and then go back to the same old habits. Give people second chances, sure. Give them the benefit of the doubt and see the best in them. But don't let people walk all over you, and don't let them talk you out of your own boundaries. Or else your body is just going to take the wheel back, because you're an unreliable driver.

When we truly start to take care of ourselves, there is no further need for resentment. It does not serve a purpose. We don't require anger to avoid a toxic person. This allows the discomfort in the body to be released, while also keeping us safe.

I used to draw and paint with my friend, to try to express that feeling in my heart. When I first put it on paper, there was a constricted heart with a green thorny vine wrapped tight around it.

A year later I drew it again, and the heart was open and free. Around the edge of the drawing was a green vine with flowers on it, giving plenty of space for the heart to breathe.

The goal was not to remove all protection. The goal was to transform resentment's volatile protection into a loving guardian that actually cares for the heart. Or at least, that's my interpretation. I don't know, though, I'm not a very good artist.

Codependents, Avoidants, and Boundaries

Codependents and avoidants struggle with boundaries more than most other types. Whenever conflict or criticism arises, they tend to feel an overwhelming dread or anxiety that makes it hard to take much action at all. I would suggest exploring that dread in therapy, because it's a reaction that probably comes from bad things happening when you tried to stand up for yourself in the past.

Healthy people are able to recognize when a situation is unfair, wrong, or inappropriate. They are able to state this or take action, and move on. On the other end of the spectrum, codependents and avoidants will feel tremendous fear and self-doubt before taking action. Then after the action, they will suffer some more. Lots of guilt and wondering if you were too harsh or unfair. They stand up for themselves so rarely that when they do, it ends up being overthought and extremely detailed, almost like giving the other person a speech.

A lot of times we don't want to hurt the other person's feelings. Some people will declare that this is just a fear of being disliked, but I'm not so sure about that. Thanks to the good graces of my last book, I am perfectly accustomed to people disliking me. That's not my fear. I think the issue was that I was overly concerned about the emotions of others, which made me project my own sensitivity onto them. And hey, maybe they *were* sensitive, but that doesn't make it my job to tailor my boundaries to appease someone else's sensitivities. When we're always thinking like this, we don't make space to include ourselves in the mix. We worry that we're being unfair, when most other people aren't preoccupied with this concern. So guess who's going to end up with the short end of the stick?

Cluster-B Abuse Survivor and Boundaries

"How have your boundaries been going?" I asked Elliot.

"Good and bad."

"How so?"

"The good part is that I'm implementing boundaries. The bad part is, she doesn't like them."

"Can you give me an example?"

"Well, the other day she started calling me a 'pussy' and a 'pathetic bitch' because I wasn't doing the dishes right apparently."

"That's a completely inappropriate reaction to doing the dishes incorrectly."

"And I finally pointed that out!" he said. "I calmly told her that she can't speak to me that way. I said it is unacceptable and I am always respectful to her."

"Go, you!"

"Thanks," he said. "But she hated that. She started crying and saying I'm just as abusive as she is. She accused me of yelling at her last week, even though I've never yelled at her."

"She's trying to prove that you're both 'equally as bad' so she doesn't have to face the shame of her own misbehavior."

"Yep! So I stayed calm and told her that's not true. She tried to interrupt and insist that it was, but I didn't accept her made-up reality. I wasn't mean or anything, I just kept repeating it wasn't true and I've always treated her with respect."

"How did she respond to that?"

He laughed. "She started trying to say that she 'forgives' me for yelling at her, so why can't I forgive her for one mistake. I told her I won't accept forgiveness for something I didn't do. I walked out and told her she can contact me at a later time if she wants to take responsibility for what she did."

"Elliot, that's incredible. How do you feel?"

"Confused and proud, I guess. You know, all my life I prided myself on being nice and compassionate. I still think I have those qualities, but I'm not interested in using them to fix people anymore. You know? I don't see myself as the selfless hero anymore—the guy who will stay and sacrifice myself, to prove I'm better than all the guys who left. In the past, I would have bought into her imaginary stories of me yelling. I would have doubted myself and worried it was true. I would have apologized for something I never did. I would have cried with her and comforted her, even though I was the one who was hurt by her comments."

"And now?"

"I just can't do it anymore," he said. "She contacted me again saying all the right things, apologizing, promising to change. . . . But we've been here before, and I know it won't last. It's like she'd rather pretend to be better than *actually* get better. She'd rather me go back to being a doormat, than just treat me with respect."

"That's great you're learning from the past, rather than getting sucked back into old loving romantic feelings."

"I still do love her, but it's in a different way than I used to. I genuinely want her to be happy, but I know that will never happen without some pretty serious therapy. In all honesty, my attempts to rescue her or absorb her drama were probably distracting her from getting the help she needs."

"So what are you going to do?"

"It's funny, you never told me to 'run,' like everyone else. But you taught me to like myself. And now that I like myself, I can't tolerate being with someone who disrespects me."

"That's the best possible reason to implement boundaries," I said.

"You know, the only way our relationship worked was when I absorbed everything. Now that I refuse to do that, everything is falling apart."

"Do you think that's a good or bad thing?"

"Well, I'm realizing that if I have boundaries and self-respect, I can never have a successful relationship with someone who has an untreated cluster-B disorder."

BPD and Boundaries

While people with BPD may struggle with implementing boundaries, they also struggle with respecting boundaries of others. If you have borderline personality disorder, this really is not your fault, so please let go of any shame you might feel about past boundary violations. A lot of BPD sufferers had caretakers who displayed an inappropriate version of "love," and this became their own blueprint for attachment with others. For example, if your caretaker took up way too much space in your life, sobbing and screaming at a small child for comfort, how were you supposed to know anything different?

When the BPD protective self is in charge, boundaries from others are seen as a bad thing—a threat—because they impede on your ability to be as close with this person as humanly possible. To *become* them. So the inappropriate stuff begins: oversharing, crisis overdrive, and episodes of rage or crying. The protective self feels offended and betrayed if someone expresses discomfort over this, or begins backing away. So instead of respecting the boundary, the protective self may actually ramp up the intensity.

While it may not be intentional, the BPD protective self is notorious for using sympathy and pity stories to manipulate itself back into control. So in response to someone's healthy boundary, it may start mentioning suicidal thoughts or manufacture a crisis to overcome the boundary. While this may give you what you want in the moment, this behavior can lead to partners and loved ones feeling a lot of guilt and obligation. The protective self may offer apologies and promises to change, only to resume the same behavior once the loved one is back. This is not a fair burden to put on someone else, and actually erodes their ability to implement strong boundaries in the future.

Respecting the boundaries of others will start to occur automatically as you begin to detach from the protective self and heal the underlying wound. Without all of your external obsession and "favorite person" habits, you will no longer be pushing yourself on others. You won't have the desire. So there are no boundaries to overcome, because you are not trying to become their entire life. And without the shame of abandonment, you are no longer perceiving it where it is not happening. You also know that even if it does happen, it's not a statement about *you*, so you are not desperately scrambling to avoid it.

Changing Life

As we deconstruct the protective self and resolve old wounds, we are likely to find some aspects of our lives that don't make as much sense as they used to. The protective self kept you on a constant quest for external things, convincing you that "one more thing" would finally make you happy. With no more protective self to satisfy, you probably don't want or need those things anymore. In fact, there's a good chance you'll find them draining and exhausting.

It's confusing to be bothered by things, people, or events that you once actively sought out. These things also tend to be unusually energy-consuming and time-consuming, because their entire purpose was to keep you distracted. This means that you may find yourself surrounded by things that stress you out, and it can take some maneuvering to create a life that better suits your changing priorities.

As my protective self began to crumble, I found myself center stage in an extremely stressful life of my own creation. Book deadlines on top of my full-time day job, mass website migration plans, relentless interpersonal conflicts from said website, along with CEO responsibilities for a new non-profit organization.

Again, these were all things that *I actively sought out.* Nobody forced me to do them. I was the *only person* excitedly pushing forward on all of these ideas. It was *my* dreams and goals that kept pushing for "bigger and more." So it was unsettling to suddenly feel stressed out and unhappy with all of the things I had worked so hard on.

On top of that, my daily thought processes had changed drastically. I no longer saw the world through a lens of "psychopaths versus good guys," which meant that old grandiose battles began to melt away, leaving me focused on uncomfortable sensations in my body.

One of the greatest shifts occurred when I began meditating on forgiveness each day. As the tension in my heart began to dissolve, I no longer felt angry about cluster-B disorders, which meant I no longer felt compelled to write grumpy articles about them. That's not to say that someone with an untreated personality disorder won't do infuriating things—I'm sure they will. But if I have the choice between focusing on something that tightens my heart or something that opens it, I'm going to go with the obvious choice.

On a similar note, I used to spend my morning walks listening to music and fantasizing about the next accomplishment or idea. About my book characters, or some future happy dream scenario. Now my morning walks are focused entirely on meditation, exploring the sensations in my heart, and building a relationship with unconditional love within myself.

The energy I once poured into my big plans was no longer available, but that didn't stop them from needing my energy. The website still had plenty of errors, my books needed to be finished, and conflicts continued to bubble up. My desire to focus on meditations and peace was sabotaged by my own grand plans.

I couldn't just abandon commitments and promises, so instead I began to slowly make some changes. I started by disabling new registrations on the website, closing the gates to more conflict and drama. Eventually, we made the entire website private. Old members could still use the forum and post, but the website became quiet for the first time in years. Finally, I worked with the team on a plan to close the non-profit, which eliminated tons of paperwork and meetings.

Slowly but surely, the stress was starting to fade away. At the time, I never thought I'd be able to escape the life I'd built for myself. But no matter what chaos we create for ourselves, it can always be rectified. It doesn't happen overnight, but it happens.

All the time I previously spent alone by the river in a fantasy world was slowly replaced by joining tennis and softball leagues. Interacting with other people, having fun, not talking about trauma or abuse anymore. Just joking around and being myself.

No matter what chaos we create for ourselves, it can always be rectified.

Our external lives tend to mirror our current values and goals. As our values and goals shift, our external lives will slowly start to reflect those changes. When healing becomes our main priority, we naturally begin to surround ourselves with resources, people, and thoughts that promote healing. We attract the very things that we pour our energy into.

This doesn't mean we need to run away from problems, move homes, or impulsively change careers. Those things are actually all signs of the protective self talking ("Just do this one thing, then you'll be happy"). Rather, we can take a more balanced approach in understanding what aspects of our lives were chosen by the protective self, and decide if they still serve us.

This can be sort of trippy at first, because you may start to doubt your own likes and dislikes. You may find yourself debating who is the "real" you versus the protective self. Don't worry too much about this or overthink it. You'll probably still enjoy plenty of the things you used to enjoy. You may just start to shift your relationship with those things.

For example, I still love my morning nature walks. They're

the best part of my day. But my focus and thoughts during the walks are completely different now. Writing is something that also started to change a lot for me. It used to be all about validation and success. I wrote because I wanted to prove myself and "make it big." But without my protective self, my writing now comes from the heart. I don't want to constantly help and rescue people anymore. I don't want to focus on everyone else's problems all the time. I simply want to explore my own challenges, and share the tools I've learned that might help others help themselves.

Codependents and Changing Life

Codependents are likely to have some of the most difficult and uncomfortable adjustments of all. In the past, you may have prided yourself on "helping" people, listening to their problems, jumping to the rescue. You were the perfect listening ear, soothing and comforting their emotions because they didn't know how to do it for themselves. You spent your free time thinking about other people's issues and feeling little bursts of excitement at the thought of saving them.

Once the protective self is gone, you're now surrounded by a lot of needy people who depend on you. Because you no longer gain self-worth from helping other people, this actually becomes draining very quickly. Maybe you had some perpetual complainers you used to cheer up by being positive and uplifting. But when you're focusing on your own issues, this type of negativity is far less endearing.

You may find yourself involved in more extreme dynamics, with addicts or disordered individuals whose dependency is much more invasive. For example, people with untreated borderline personality disorder may be calling you sobbing on a regular basis and sharing unending crisis stories. Every time you think you've resolved one issue, they're leaning on you for help with a new trauma. They may even discuss suicide or self-harm with you, which makes you feel afraid and obligated to keep helping. These life-and-death situations (which also occur with addiction and alcoholism) can keep you stuck in frightening dynamics.

As you begin to back away from these situations and set boundaries, there's a good chance people will struggle to restore the old dynamic, because it suited them. They may use crisis-manufacturing, guilt-tripping, manipulation, and even intimidation. They might accuse you of being selfish or mean, for being less easygoing about their inappropriate behavior. This is all just an attempt to restore the relationship that worked fine—for them.

Keep in mind, at some point this dynamic suited you too. You may have gotten some enjoyment out of helping others and playing therapist, so it makes sense that the people you helped would continue to seek support from you. With this perspective, it's easier to let go of any resentment you might carry about getting stuck in these situations. You don't need to be unkind or dismissive in setting boundaries, you can simply let others know that this dynamic seems unhealthy, you need some space to work on yourself, and perhaps you could both benefit from some therapy.

If someone reacts to a diplomatic statement like this with venom or intimidation or guilt, then you can be even firmer in your resolve that this person is no longer a good fit. You cannot control their reactions, but you can protect yourself from dynamics that don't work for you.

When you stop feeling attracted to people who need rescuing, your relationships naturally become more fulfilling. It's not that these people don't deserve saving, it's just that you come to understand that *you* are not the source of that saving. It never works. Instead of selecting partners based on who they *could* be (if they just accepted all of your love and took all your advice), you select partners based on who they are *right now*. Pity is not the same thing as love. Another nice change is that you'll start feeling more comfortable asking for what you want. You might be the kind of person who secretly wishes for a raise every year because you worked really hard and hope that somebody will notice. With codependency, you feel too guilty or embarrassed to ask directly, and instead just hope someone else will offer it to you. When they don't, you feel disappointed and unappreciated.

But when you stop feeling guilty and ashamed of your needs, you'll be able to stick up for what you deserve. You're no longer trying to be "nice" and "agreeable" all the time, because that doesn't work for you anymore. Standing up for your needs isn't going to result in automatic rejection or people thinking you're crazy.

At the core of codependency, there is this sense that nothing you ever do is good enough. But the real problem is that this causes you to *listen* to people who tell you that you're not good enough, thereby reinforcing the inner voice. You think they must know something you don't, that their negativity must secretly be right, because it just seems so convincing (because it's reaffirming a secret belief you have of yourself).

Once I saw this, I finally stopped feeling shortchanged and undervalued all the time, because I became able to advocate for myself when the situation called for it. I stopped tiptoeing around everyone else's feelings and instead just trusted that my decisions were fair.

Once we start valuing ourselves, we naturally gravitate toward others who value us as well.

Cluster-B Survivor and Changing Life

In the immediate aftermath of a cluster-B relationship, survivors tend to feel like they've lost the best thing that ever happened to them. They may even try to re-create the intense and passionate dynamic with future partners, only to become frustrated when it repeatedly does not work.

But once we turn our attention inward, we start to realize that the old intense relationship dynamic isn't even desirable anymore; and if it were to present itself again, you'd say, "No, thanks." It's not just the abuse that you're resistant to, but the overly dramatic, overly validating, overly attention-seeking, overly flattering, overly communicative, overly everything. Things which, at some point, were the very foundation of the relationship you previously pined for.

This can be an unsettling shift, discovering that "the best thing that ever happened" is no longer of any interest to you.

You may find that you enjoy the peace and quiet of a single life, without constant intensity and passion. And if you choose to pursue relationships again, you're likely to find yourself seeking out qualities that were not present in your cluster-B relationship: consistency, stability, security, harmony, authenticity, communication. It's no longer just a big romantic love-bomb with two people telling each other how great they are. It's no longer about being "perfect" or "flawless." It's no longer exciting to have someone's attention laser-focused on you. It's no longer flattering to have someone be obsessed with you.

When we have low self-esteem or fears of rejection, cluster-B personalities can immediately quell all of those fears. Their automatic fascination with us makes us feel important, and 100 percent safe from rejection. We can skip past all of the nervous "getting to know you" steps, and dive straight into a passionate romantic relationship. They idealize you, flatter you, "attach" quickly, obsess over you, immediately desire you, praise you above all others—they "love" you, when they do not even know who you are.

The trouble, of course, is that people who "attach" so quickly will also "detach" just as quickly. They will idealize and obsess over other people during your actual relationship. Because the type of attachment they gave *you* was superficial and not unique to you.

When we replace old, heavy, and sad feelings of longing with the spiritual sensations of unconditional love, we start meeting our own needs. We don't look to others for a fairy-tale romance, so we stop attracting that initial intensity that once felt like "love." We don't just fall for the people who make us feel safe from rejection by their initial obsession with us, because then our entire relationship is dictated by their changing perceptions of us.

Especially for people recovering from borderline relationships, you are likely to find that your inner rescuer has disappeared. In the past, you may have heard sympathetic stories in the early phases of dating, about their life of abuse or the void inside of them or traumatic childhood or cheating ex. Back then you may have jumped in to comfort them, save the day, soothe them, and feel a heavy longing in your heart to save them. But as you start to work through and resolve your own issues, this old role becomes much less appealing.

It's not that you become heartless and stop caring about the suffering of others. It's simply that you recognize that people need to work through their own issues to find happiness. And acting as a security blanket for another human being only serves to delay them from getting to that point. A partner can be supportive and helpful, but you're not meant to be someone else's crutch. And certainly when you feel like a crutch in the early days of dating, this is at best a warning sign that the person is not ready for a relationship.

On a similar note, people who have been through cluster-B relationships tend to spend a lot of time researching the disorders and learning about their behaviors. Most survivors could practically have a psychology degree by the time they start feeling better. I'm not suggesting that these lessons won't remain helpful in your future endeavors, but as you begin to give yourself unconditional love, all of the analyzing and trying to understand someone else's mind—all of that external focus—becomes less interesting or relevant.

One of the most active sections of the Psychopath Free forum was called "Tell Your Story," which I still think is a very important part of early recovery. However, I believe a big part of healing is actually about *detaching from* the story. When we're wounded, the story carries a great deal of importance because it helps us piece together a very chaotic situation. But as we experience and release our wound, the story really loses its meaning. Yes, it happened and, yes, it was traumatizing. But it didn't really have anything to do with us, which is one of the strangest things to understand. Once we realize this, our attachment to the story starts to dissolve because it is not who we are.

When we detach from the story, we also start to detach from the resources we once relied upon to solidify our story. I know this sounds silly coming from a cofounder of PsychopathFree .com and author of *Psychopath Free*, but really—what I want most for you is to never need any of my resources again. Stay for the community and friendships, but trust your intuition and your reality so that you do not need to be thinking about psychopaths all day to keep yourself safe. I relied so heavily upon others to validate my story because I had lost the ability to trust myself. Once I regained this, my interest in sharing my story disappeared.

Finally, I think cluster-B survivors have a big challenge with resentment. The nature of cluster-B disorders tends to result in a lot of lying, deceit, betrayal, blame, infidelity, hypocrisy, and projection. There is rarely ever any genuine apology or remorse. They constantly blame their victims for their own misbehavior. Survivors find themselves engaged in constant mental battles long after the abuse has ended. Resentment is not only understandable, but expected. I hope that the tools I have provided about resentment and forgiveness can help you to release these (very valid) feelings.

When we carry wounds and resentments, every "new" bad thing that happens tends to add on to the existing pain and frustration. This snowballs bigger and bigger until it becomes suffocating, because life inevitably continues to throw challenges our way. When the old wound and resentment dissolve, challenges continue to happen, but they don't have anything to land on anymore. There is no more concept of "this happened, on top of everything else that already happened." The natural flow and release of life events is restored.

BPD and Changing Life

In their frantic efforts to avoid deep feelings of rejection and worthlessness, people with BPD tend to act out impulsively and make abrupt decisions. Coupled with their constantly changing identities, this can lead to a life fraught with chaos and instability.

As you begin to observe the protective self and notice how it relentlessly suggests these impulsive life changes, you stop taking its commands as truth. Instead, you learn to slow down and stay with the discomfort that arises when you don't make these big changes. As you stop looking for external reasons to explain your discomfort, you eventually come face-to-face with the real problem. You start to identify less with chaos and change.

For example, those with BPD may find themselves in considerable debt from their changing goals and spending sprees. As they begin this work, they may realize they are content with a stable career, even if it's not their "dream job." They may look back and regret all of the time and money they poured into so many changing identities, wishing they could hit the "reset" button and start fresh with this new stable life.

But as I mentioned, change is slow, and even the most frightening issues can be resolved with enough time. Setting up a steady plan to pay off your debt can help you learn fiscal responsibility and healthier spending habits. Typically, people with BPD carry a deep-down shame about their spending issues or other impulsive behaviors, but their protective self keeps them from exploring it. This leads to more distractions, more spending, and more shame.

As you become aware of the protective self and stop the loop, you become okay with exploring the underlying shame. It doesn't consume you. You can accept the possibility that you have been reckless with money, without believing you're a bad or irredeemable person. You can begin to learn from your mistakes and make improvements for the future, because mistakes no longer equate to "I'm defective and bad."

On a similar note, relationships have likely been a rocky road, starting out extremely intense and passionate, but ending catastrophically. The protective self has used relationships and "favorite people" to distract you from pain, to fill its void and feel loved. Like a drug, it latched on to other people for dear life.

This constant need for sympathy and attention made sense

when you were living through the protective self. But as you explore and release your resistances to unconditional love, you will begin to realize that no amount of external sympathy or attention could ever overcome the resistances in your body. You are the only person who can do the hard work to free yourself. And in doing so, you end up having a much different perspective on relationships.

When you restore your own inner light, you no longer require the energy of others to feel alive. I don't know how to explain this, but your body will rush with a sense of vitality that just washes away all of your old fears, rejections, and shames. Without those things, you are not constantly looking to others for validation. You are generating your love from within. It becomes less about "proving" love or idealizing others, and more about just freely sharing this new part of yourself with others.

In the past, you always wanted to make sure others saw you as the tragic victim. This was the best way you knew how to receive comfort and sympathy. But as you experience a different type of love surge through your body, you will find yourself no longer interested in that old dynamic. You were trying to fill an old void with sympathy, but you are not the void anymore. This naturally attracts much healthier partners, whereas your old needs would have attracted codependents and narcissists.

There is no more need to be "right" or rewrite history or "win" games. It's no longer about being perfect and flawless all the time, so when you make missteps, you do not feel an overwhelming shame that must be avoided. In the past, this shame caused you to contract and create elaborate stories to disprove your shame. But now you are making healthier, smarter decisions without that constant nagging fear that you're evil or bad.

Without this nagging fear also comes a great relief—you don't have to be "perfect" anymore. The inner drive to present this perfect mirror of others naturally diminishes as your focus shifts from external to internal. Rather than shifting between "perfect" and episode and shame, you have learned how to stay on the same wavelength as your shame. You have learned to tolerate this discomfort so you could finally release your core wounding. Without the core wounding, there is no further need for this cycle. There is no need to be perfect, and no bubbling shame that inevitably sabotages the perfection.

Additionally, rejection no longer triggers the inner wound. You can experience rejection without desperately trying to avoid it, because it's not bringing you back to that sense of defectiveness. A breakup no longer brings you back to intolerable sensations of abandonment. That's not to say breakups and rejections will feel great, but you won't need to organize your life around avoiding them anymore.

Finally, one of the biggest changes for individuals with BPD is their identity. You may have been looking your whole life for an identity, finding that it always escapes you even when you were sure it was "the one." That's because your true identity has been locked away by the protective self. The more you do this work, the more you will find the true parts of yourself that have been missing. It's no longer an external search for purpose, but rather a discovery of the truth in your own body.

When you stop avoiding and resisting that truth, you can

finally acknowledge and heal it. Life becomes so much calmer. It is no longer a manic search for meaning, filled with shaky declarations of personality and passions. Your identity is no longer a never-ending quest to prove "I am," but rather an exploration into your suffering so that you can let go of what you "are not." Once you do that, your true self comes rushing back in at last.

C-PTSD and Changing Life

C-PTSD sufferers may find less of an adjustment than other types, because they have already been living somewhat low-risk lives. Their protective self's distractions have been largely in the mind: Fantasies of justice or revenge, ruminating and resenting, and sharing stories with other survivors. Obsessively interested in politics, conspiracies, and injustice. Any big-picture dynamic that has a "bad guy" versus "good guy."

Perhaps the biggest transition is a dwindling interest in suffering and trauma. It can be very unsettling to lose interest in these topics, when they may have comprised a large part of your time and social life. But as the trauma leaves you, you no longer identify with it. The perpetrator, who once seemed a dominating and frightening figure, isn't really on your mind anymore, because you no longer identify as their dominated and frightened victim. The connection they forged with you is dissolving. The messages they left behind are losing their weight.

When we don't carry such intense suffering inside us anymore, we tend to turn toward lighter things. Of course we may still have a desire to help others, but it's no longer consuming our entire life. We may feel ready for a new hobby, a team sport, a fun pet, or a loving relationship. As we pour our energy into those things, we find our general mood lightens drastically. It's easier to just laugh and have fun again, without thinking of the past injustices that occurred.

Similar to codependents, you may find yourself surrounded by a lot of hurting people who need your help. You might have a blog, exchange e-mails with other survivors, or help to moderate some type of support group. Unfortunately, it's common for these dynamics to be filled with drama, anger, paranoia, and splitting (where people go from seeing you as a "beautiful soul healer" to "worse than their abuser"). None of these things are a reflection on you, it's just a lot of wounded people who don't know what to do with their wounds.

As we turn our attention inward, we become more comfortable with the idea of letting others do the same thing. There is no longer a desire to control or rescue, but rather a newfound faith that people can find their own path to peace.

When we're constantly at war with the world, the world ends up fighting back. These issues are almost like clockwork: First, someone is grieving and suffering an intense pain. Next, they take on a very polarized position about that suffering, based exclusively on pointing out the *cause* of the suffering (the "bad other"). This is often about "raising awareness" or "exposure" or "preventing others from experiencing the same suffering."

Inevitably, this polarized position attracts more and more resistance from the other end of the spectrum (the other pole).

The "bad other" feels attacked and persecuted, so they begin to feel like *your* victim. Before you know it, life becomes a daily battle. Everyone's accusing the other of lying, gaslighting, playing the victim, victim blaming, projection, mental gymnastics, and smear campaigns. Nobody's convincing the other of anything, they're just arguing about the argument itself. Everyone's constantly outraged, bitter, and mocking one another.

This is more or less what our modern political climate has become. A battle of persecution and victimhood. People provoking each other, and then saying *"See?"* when the other person reacts. Assuming the worst of the other "side" based on the divisive rhetoric of their fringe—generalizing an entire ideology based on tweets from random jerks on the Internet.

We forget the quiet majority that have far more in common with us.

Shifting from a Dual to Non-Dual Perspective

So much of what we learn about love is taught by people who never really loved us.

—R. H. SIN

The more time we spend deconstructing the protective self and becoming aware of its tricks, the less and less we identify with it. The same becomes true for the core wound that lives underneath it. We put a lot of energy into offering it love and comfort, which is a great way to soften the body and build our unconditional love. But when we comfort the wound, we are accepting and nurturing it as a part of ourselves that needs help.

The problem here is that the core wound is *not* who we are.

This is a really important concept, but also confusing to explain.

You can spend a lifetime trying to "heal" or "soothe" toxic shame, but this is not the best approach, because toxic shame is a false message absorbed from external events.

So what is the purpose of nurturing something that is not who you are? As long as the core wound remains a part of our psyche, we are still trying to disprove it. We are saying: "No, I'm not rejectable" or "Yes, I'm a good person." These things are true, but who are we arguing with? And why doesn't this argument ever seem to end?

The argument never ends because the core wound is a persistent sensation. A sensation that says you are [not enough/ worthless/inadequate/rejectable/evil/unwanted].

When we comfort or explain energy, we perpetuate it.

As long as you try to disprove it, your life is still organized around the premise that it was true. How can you heal something if it is not even who you are? If you try to heal it, you are accepting that it is a part of who you are, which it is not.

Instead, Stephen Wolinsky offers a different solution: you need to realize that it is not who you are, and "un-be" it. He describes these wounds in the context of quantum psychology. I know that sounds confusing, but it's actually really simple. The idea is that all wounds are simply energy stored in the body. Energy. Nothing more and nothing less. Energy can either be perpetuated or dissolved. When we comfort or explain energy, we perpetuate it. When we un-identify with it, it dissolves.

Wolinsky further explains, "You cannot heal a False Conclusion, because it is False. You must 'see' the False Conclusion as a False Conclusion and discard it. You can never overcome or heal your False Core, you can only be free of it by realizing it is not you."

So if you experience a painful sensation of "I am bad," the long-term solution is not to soothe that feeling or repeatedly tell yourself "No, I am good!" This might have temporary effects, but it will never last, because it is still trying to disprove a false message. Instead, we dismiss the entire idea of "I am bad." It is not who we are, so it does not need to be healed or soothed. It needs to be dismissed from our identity.

For example, if I say, "You are a llama," will you now spend your entire life introducing yourself to people by saying: "Hello, I am *not* a llama. I am a human"? Of course not. You know you're not a llama. It's such a goofy thing for me to even suggest, so you don't need to bother explaining to anyone (especially yourself) that you're not a llama.

Toxic shame is equally as untrue and goofy. The problem is that toxic shame is much more sneaky and parasitic than accusations of being a llama. It sneaks into you and hangs on for dear life, tricking you and scaring you, convincing you that it is the "ultimate truth." It clings on to the old rejection to give itself some semblance of control over preventing the shame from ever happening again. It is the body's attempt to function in a harsh world where your own love was once rejected and unwanted.

We've established that you do not walk around saying "I am a human," because you already know you're a human, not a llama. However, you may constantly try to prove to yourself and others "I am adequate" or "I am enough," which only really makes sense if you believe you are *in*adequate or *not* enough. So the solution is not to keep telling ourselves we are the opposite of our wound. The solution is to stop identifying with the wound altogether. Instead of striving for "I am enough," you drop the belief of "I am not enough."

Author Robert Burney wrote, "We use external things—success, looks, productivity, substances—to try to cover up, overcome, make up for, the personal defectiveness that we felt caused our hearts to be broken and our souls wounded. And that personal defectiveness is a lie."

This feeling of toxic shame cannot be healed, coddled, or comforted—because it was never true to begin with. It sneaked inside of you a long time ago, like a parasite, and it has been living there rent-free ever since. And it will stay inside of you for as long as you're willing to entertain its dark and persuasive message. This work is about realizing that the wound wasn't even true, so there is no further need to organize our lives around preventing or disproving it.

Instead of trying to heal the wound, try imagining the wound as me calling you a llama. Imagine it carries *exactly* that much importance and truth. I know this isn't the most spiritual meditation in the world, but I've found it really helpful for minimizing the power that the wound carries. It almost becomes funny, which is indeed a helpful antidote to shame.

People say that peace comes from acceptance, but you must not accept toxic shame. You can accept that it's your current state of being, but you must work toward releasing it from your psyche. It does not belong there.

When we comfort this wound, we are approaching things from a dual perspective. The two parts of this duality are "shameful, hurting me" and "unconditional love, which comforts shameful, hurting me." The dual perspective automatically means we are separate from the unconditional love. It says we are the wounded suffering individual, and unconditional love is the *separate* thing helping us.

I think this is the natural path when we begin to discover our own suffering and we wish to heal it. We offer ourselves the same love we might hope to receive from a partner or parent. But in doing so, we solidify our identity as the thing needing help. This is why I eventually discourage the constant storytelling and psychological analysis of why we are suffering.

I have found this path leads to a dead end. We need to tell ourselves a new story.

We need to tell ourselves a new story.

This is where the non-dual perspective comes into play. If we begin to un-identify with the wound inside of us, we no longer have anything to heal or comfort. But if the shame is not our true self, then what is?

What about the unconditional love that has been guiding us through this journey?

When we let go of the tension and resistances in the body that arise from shame, unconditional love automatically comes rushing back in. It has been there the whole time, there were just things inside of our bodies and minds that blocked it out.

This is not a matter of consciously declaring "I am unconditional love." You'll get some funny looks if you walk down the street shouting that. It is simply what happens when you let go of the protective self and the underlying toxic shame. When you remove all resistances to love, love comes back home to you where it belongs. It is our natural state of being, how we are intended to exist. And so it is less about declaring "I am" and more about letting go of what you are not. The "I am" comes naturally from there.

Things like shame, rejection, humiliation, guilt, resentment, and fear are all blockers. They tense parts of our body and keep out the love. As my brother once told me, "The sun is always there. You might not be able to see it on a cloudy day, but that doesn't mean the sun has gone away. It just means you can't see it."

Letting Go of Separation

With the non-dual perspective, there are no longer two players involved. There is no healer and sufferer. There is no separation between you and unconditional love. It is you. You are it. It is all of us. Of course it is who we are. It came from our own brains, as the antidote to the suffering in that same brain. How *cool* is that?

We just sometimes carry things inside of us that shut out the love. And perhaps a big part of life is about identifying those resistances and releasing them, so we can be free.

There are many great meditations and prayers that can help you accomplish this. One visualization that helps me a lot is to imagine the core wound is in my hands (rather than wrapped around my heart). When I hold it out in front of me, I can see it writhing and clawing, desperately clinging to control. It's not a part of me anymore, but instead just an old energy that was born from fear. It is not who I am.

Try imagining your wound in your hands, across the room, or dissolved altogether. This can take a lot of time and practice. Listen to the voices and fears that try to keep you inextricably linked to your wound, making it seemingly impossible to disconnect from it. Those are all just last-ditch efforts from the wound to keep its place in you.

Another way to approach this perspective is to experiment with what it would feel like if this original shaming or rejection or betrayal *hadn't* happened to you. What if it had happened to some other person? What would your body feel like then? In the spiritual sense, you are only love—the things that happen(ed) to you here on Earth are the result of a hostile place full of wounded people. They may have passed along their wounds to you, but those wounds don't change who you *actually* are. The wound's default response to this may be: "But it *did* happen! It's an important part of who I am." While I of course respect every-one's lived experience, my question is: Does identifying with this story bring suffering or happiness? If it brings only suffering, why not try un-identifying with it?

Some people ask, "If I'm un-identifying with my own experience, then aren't I just numbing and dissociating like the protective self did?" But the difference here is that instead of your body numbing out pain as a subconscious work-around, you are consciously using mindfulness to fully experience pain and let it go. There are no distractions. You will feel no numbness. Only light.

You may even find that there's a part of you that is hesitant to let go of this wound that causes you so much misery. Because if you don't hold on to this pain, you may not be hyperaware of when it might happen again. And that's true. You are no longer organizing your life around avoiding pain, which means that pain could happen again. Your most authentic self could be met with disgust or rejection again. The difference is, without the wound, this pain will not trigger any sense of inner defectiveness again.

There is also a fear of the unknown. The wound almost brings us a sense of control and comfort—a familiar way to organize and process the world around us. Who will we become if we stop identifying with this thing that has operated our lives for the past however many years? The truth is, we don't know. But we *do* know something—we know that our current state does not feel good. It may have kept us relatively functional, but it is not how we are supposed to feel. And so it takes a leap of faith, and a willingness to relinquish the control that comes with holding on to suffering.

When you stop identifying as the suffering one, the old toxic

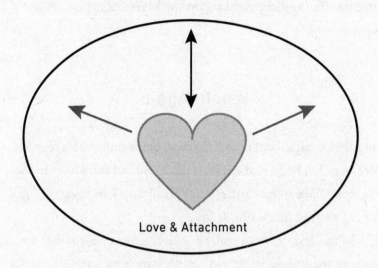

sludge is replaced by a lightness and freedom surging through the body. For me, it felt like mind, body, and spirit reunited. I had forgotten what it was like to feel love and joy for no reason. It was a physical sensation through my heart, tingling and dissolving, flooding with a sensation I cannot describe with words. Heavy things like depression and anxiety were like distant dreams—they no longer even made sense to me.

Once this connection is restored, our diagram looks more like the one above.

Instead of a wounded protective self absorbing external measures of worth to stay alive, we have restored our connection with love, and radiate it outward. We've gone from a black hole to a source of light.

As I felt my body light up, I wondered: How could the source of my suffering—the tightness in my heart—also be a source of such magic?

Whole Again

This book started out with a fracture, but it ends with a reunion. When mind, body, and spirit are disconnected from one another we experience untold suffering. When they join together once again, we find indescribable joy.

In the end, it is not really a search for love, but rather a release of the things inside us that block us from love—the resistances and wounds. Once those are gone, the love comes rushing back inside on its own.

So the fracture isn't really a fracture at all. When we think of a fracture, we think of broken glass. To fix broken glass, you have to glue or tape the pieces back together. Even after it's mended, it's always broken. This is not the case with the human heart.

In Hindu traditions, the heart is known as *anahata*, which translates literally to "unstruck." So many of us believe that our hearts have been permanently broken because of our life experiences, but it's that *belief* of brokenness that causes us suffering. Underneath it all is still just love, unstruck by any of this. And it is always trying to get out and radiate for the world.

In the end, that is the protective self's greatest fear: unconditional love. The last time we knew unconditional love, it was followed by emotional chaos, rejection, and suffering. And so the protective self was born not only to protect the resulting wound, but to block the love. Love that washes everything else away and allows us to return to our bodies in the present moment. Love that is so overwhelmingly powerful that we seem to lose our control if we let it come back. But control over what? Having it rejected again? So we pre-reject ourselves all the time, in hopes that we beat others to the punch.

The paradox is, unconditional love does not know or care about rejection. So if we accept it as our true identity, and give up the wounded identity, then there is nothing left to fear. If someone harms us, it is a reflection of their demons, not our own. Therefore, it doesn't have to stick to us or wound us, because it is not who we are.

Of course we must take measures to avoid intentional betrayal, set boundaries, and trust our intuition. Otherwise, we are just setting ourselves up for failure and disappointment. But we can do this with a loving presence that wants the best for us, rather than clinging to tight resentment and rejection around the heart to keep us protected. Those old protective mechanisms ironically seem to attract more of the same hurt and reinforce the need for protection, while love guides us down different paths.

Once our wounds begin to heal and dissolve, it all starts to seem so obvious. A lot of people grieve for all the time lost, wondering why they spent so much of their life in darkness when this light was available the whole time. But there's really nothing to grieve. It's part of the human experience, and we've found our way home.

None of the steps could have been skipped. You couldn't have just gone from numb to love, because the pain had to be un-numbed in order to find the love. The wound had to come out one way or another. In the time we spent with the wound, we learned patience and compassion—not the type of savior compassion that can be exploited, but a genuine understanding and empathy for the human condition.

I agree that it does seem a bit circuitous to spend all this time becoming aware of the protective self, only to decide that isn't who we are, and then un-numbing a wound, only to decide that's not who we are either. But in order to release shame, we have to learn how to tolerate the discomfort it causes in our bodies. And in doing so, we learn so many important things about ourselves, and we gain a great deal of compassion along the way. The end result is infinitely better than remaining in the numb trance of the protective self.

The protective self looks back and thinks everything would have worked fine if everything just went right, if people just behaved correctly, if relationships just worked out, if *X* just happened. But it seems the universe is always conspiring to ensure *X* does *not* happen, because the protective self is *destined to fail*. If the protective self is given everything it wants, then it remains in control, temporarily satisfied, and blocked away from the most important parts of being human.

So all experiences, *especially* the failures, are responsible for bringing us to this exact moment. There is no further need to grieve or wish things had gone differently. There is no further need to feel unfairly betrayed or wronged. We didn't need a prettier path to this point, because the unprettiness is exactly what got us here. Had we been given everything we wanted, we'd still be living in the trance of the protective self. Some of the world's greatest gifts are the opposite of what we think we want most.

Throughout this book, you've developed your unconditional love. It grew stronger as you suffered more, so it could carry everything. It gave you faith and encouragement when you had none. It deflects fear and self-doubt like flies. It never stops loving you, even (especially) when you stumble.

That is who you truly are: your Spirit. The thing you lost long ago, when it locked away the pain in your body to protect you. By forgiving it for this action, you allow it back home in your body and the reunion is complete. Even when you were disconnected, it stayed with you always. Waiting for you to find it. Banging on the doors of consciousness, maybe even showering you with fear and pain so that you could finally find it again.

Now all you need to do is let it back inside.

Afterword

Angel

Since *Psychopath Free* was published, our kitties sadly passed away from old age. A year later, around Thanksgiving time, my family adopted a new cat from the shelter nearby. Her name is Angel and she came from a really rough background.

She was in a hoarding situation for three years and had multiple litters of kittens. She was mistreated and had a big scar on her arm when we found her. We originally didn't even see her at the shelter. We had been there for an hour and we were about to leave, when I noticed a quivering gray lump in the back of one of the cages we earlier thought was empty.

I reached my hand in and petted her a few times. She started out very tense and didn't budge from her spot. But within a few minutes, she transformed into a purry love ball, stretching out her arms and exposing her belly, which was freshly shaved for her spaying surgery. Between the surgery, the shelter, the hoarding house, and the kittens, she had clearly been through a lot.

My mom and I immediately fell in love with her and applied to adopt her. The shelter warned us that she might be extremely shy and hide from us most of the time, and they were correct. When we got home, the first thing she did was sprint under the couch. She stayed there for the rest of the day, until we managed to lure her into the bathroom, where we had put her cat food, litter box, and a cozy cat bad.

Every time someone walked toward her, she would tense up and make herself as small as possible. She was obviously very afraid of people. I knew I should have just left her alone, but I'm obnoxious with cats. So when everyone went to sleep, I picked her up and brought her to the couch with me. She panicked at first, but I just kept repeating, "It's okay, you're safe" and made her a protected area between me and the cushions.

Within a few minutes, she calmed down and flopped over. Next came the purring. Then the face-butting into my hands. She fell asleep in my arms in what seemed to be her first real sleep in ages. I didn't want to disturb her, so I stayed up most of the night petting her and watching *American Ninja Warrior*.

Over the next few weeks she slowly began to adjust to her new life. She took a quick liking to my mom, and she loved batting at toys that my dad waved around for her. But any time there was a noise nearby, even a small one, she would jump up and dart away. You could feel it in her body, a constant quivering tension and alertness, even when she was relaxing.

Of course this tension was not something that any animal

should have to live with, but at some point in her life, it was necessary for her survival. And that protective guard remained with her, even when she was safe from harm. From our first night together, I learned that she loved being in safe, confined spots, so I'd build her pillow forts with blankets where she was covered on all sides. As soon as she entered them, she'd relax and become snuggly again.

I made these pillow forts in every room that she entered, and she'd immediately run into them and hide. My dad called me a feline enabler. Probably true.

But by Christmastime, everything changed. These days she hops up to the couch on her own, wanders around the house like she owns the place, and no longer needs pillow forts to keep her safe. Right now, she's sitting in my lap by the fireplace, stretched out and purring, kneading the air without a care in the world. She doesn't even notice when people come in with their clunky winter boots and close the door loudly behind them.

Life can dish out scary and unfair experiences—traumas that seem to take control of our lives. Our bodies try to help us, staying hypervigilant to prevent the same thing from ever happening again, but this comes at a great cost. When we're in a constant state of heightened awareness, we are unable to relax and be vulnerable in the present moment. Everything feels like a threat, even the things that are trying to help us.

In the presence of unconditional love and consistent kindness, we can experiment with letting down our guard so that we can finally tend to our wounds. The amazing thing about human consciousness is that we're able to offer this unconditional love to *ourselves.* Of course it makes a big difference to be in a safe environment with support from loved ones and professionals, but no matter where life takes us and no matter our surroundings, we can access this love. The more time we spend in its presence, the more we melt and come in touch with the truth that lives in our bodies.

Once we start this process, everything becomes lighter. Without old wounds inside of us, we are free to live our lives more playfully and humorously. We take things less seriously and feel grateful for the little things.

These days, Angel spends most of her days playing with toys, running around, and taking naps. Sometimes I think back to when she needed pillow forts to feel safe, but I know she is so much happier now. She is her true self—who she was meant to be.

And that is what I wish for every reader of this book. No more pillow forts. Just the freedom to play around, be frisky, and snuggle.

That's how it's supposed to be.

ACKNOWLEDGMENTS

Thank you—to so many people, for so many reasons:

Mom and Dad, for raising me with love and humor, giving me the blueprints to find my way home.

Lydia, Doug, and Joely, for sharing all the wisdom you've learned along the way, and for always making me laugh.

Grandma, Jane, Ninny, Poppa, Cathy, Mike, Greg, Cara, Ted, Jo, Hannah, Grayce, and Daniel, for all of the wonderful memories, stories, and dinners. I love our family so much.

Emmanuelle and Marian, for believing in this project and working so hard to help people in need. You both inspire me more than words can express. Thank you also to Dorian Hastings, for your incredible copyediting skills. You caught things I never would have noticed in a million years.

Ben, for your smile, which makes me smile.

The Psychopath Free team and members, for hanging on

through quite a wild ride and becoming the best friends a person could ask for.

Shannon, for writing the beautiful foreword for this book, and for all that you do to help abuse survivors. I cannot wait to see you in Mexico someday!

Akamai, for the friends and mentors who make every day fun and challenging. Thank you for allowing me to balance my technical and creative lives.

Bubbles and Tennis4All, for all of the outdoor athletic adventures that make me happy and unusually social.

Jan Steele, for the letter you mailed me. Thank you for nurturing the hearts and creative minds of so many students. I miss you so much.

Friends and family, there are too many to mention. I love you so much, and I cannot believe how lucky I am to experience this life surrounded by such good people.

And finally, thank you to all of the people in the psychological, spiritual, and creative fields who pour their time and energy into making the world a better place—into helping people find peace. Without your research and insights, this book would not have been possible.

ABOUT THE AUTHOR

Jackson MacKenzie has worked with thousands of abuse survivors and perpetrators around the world. He hosts a lively Facebook page (Psychopath Free) aimed at helping readers identify and heal from traumatic situations. His first book, *Psychopath Free*, is a leading resource on toxic relationship recovery. When he's not writing, MacKenzie works as a technical analyst in Boston. You can most likely find him out by a river, lake, pool, or some other body of water.